To:_____

From:_____

THE WICKED WIT OF
CHARLES DICKENS

THE WICKED WIT OF
CHARLES DICKENS

Compiled, edited and introduced by

Shelley Klein

Michael O'Mara Books Limited

This revised edition first published in Great Britain in 2011 by
Michael O'Mara Books Limited
9 Lion Yard
Tremadoc Road
London SW4 7NQ

A CIP catalogue record for this book is available
from the British Library

ISBN 978-1-84317-568-1

1 3 5 7 9 10 8 6 4 2

Designed and typeset by Design 23

Printed and bound in Great Britain by Clays Ltd, St Ives plc

Contents

Introduction

Born at 387 Mile End Terrace, Landport, in Portsea, on 7 February 1812 (seven years after Nelson defeated Napoleon at the Battle of Trafalgar, and seven years before the birth of Queen Victoria), Charles Dickens was not only a child of the nineteenth century but also became one of its greatest social and political commentators. His early years were to all intents and purposes happy ones, for, as G. K. Chesterton wrote, 'He fell into the family . . . during one of its comfortable periods, and he never in those early days thought of himself as anything but as a comfortable middle-class child, the son of a comfortable middle-class man.' In fact, his father, John Dickens, was at the time of Charles's birth a clerk in the Naval Pay Office at Portsmouth, a job that obliged the family to move from naval port to naval port during the first ten years of the young Charles's life.

The second of eight children (six of whom survived) Charles was immediately recognized to be an exceptionally bright child (indeed some have surmised that he had a photographic memory). He enjoyed singing and performing and his father often took him to taverns where he would stand Charles on a table in order that he could perform. However, although family life was happy, it did have a dark side, for the fact was that Mr and Mrs Dickens had a penchant for living beyond their means.

When Charles was ten years old, the family moved once more, this time to London. The move to 16 Bayham Street, Camden Town – at that time nothing more than a dreary suburb – was coupled with a decrease in John Dickens's pay, which meant that the family now had a struggle to keep their heads above water. It was at this point that Charles received the first major shock of his life, for rather than being enrolled in school, he was instead expected to do odd jobs around the house and run errands.

Suddenly Charles's idyllic childhood was over – a fact that must have had a major effect upon the young Dickens – while the mounting debts that his parents were accruing (they had to sell the family furniture), no doubt added to his insecurity. At this point, Elizabeth Dickens tried to start up a small school, which she called 'Mrs Dickens's Establishment'. However, as Dickens later wrote, it was not a success: 'Nobody ever came to the school, nor do I recollect that anybody ever proposed to come, or that the least preparation was made to receive anybody . . .' Thus the school failed and Charles was found a job. James Lamert, a family friend, secured Charles a position at Warren's Blacking Warehouse, a shoe polish factory that stood at the edge of the River Thames at Hungerford Stairs. Aged twelve, earning six shillings a week, Charles's job was to paste labels onto the pots of shoe polish. The hours he worked were from 8 a.m. to 8 p.m. with a one-hour dinner break and a half-hour tea break. The job was both humiliating and tedious and the warehouse itself was a loathsome building, damp and overrun with rats. To make matters worse, on 24 February 1824, just a few days after he had started the job, Dickens's father was arrested and sent to the Marshalsea Debtors' Prison in Southwark.

In later years both these experiences, that of the blacking factory and of the Marshalsea Prison, provided Dickens with a great deal of material on which to base his fiction (most notably *David Copperfield* and *Little Dorrit*), but at the time it can only be imagined how crushing and desperate these events were, not to mention how perilous it must have made life seem to the young boy. Dickens's mother and siblings accompanied his father and went to live inside the prison in one small room, while Charles was sent into lodgings beside the prison and continued to work at the blacking factory. It was a terrible time. Mrs Dickens tried to keep her family going by pawning what little jewellery she had left, and the odd piece of cutlery, while Charles trudged backwards and forwards between his lodgings and his workplace. At night he read and re-read his old books – novels such as *Tom Jones* and *Robinson Crusoe*, wonderful adventure stories, which not only gave the young boy comfort, but also influenced him and gave him something to dream about.

It is estimated that Dickens spent a year working at Warren's until by a stroke of good fortune, John Dickens came into a small inheritance. On 26 April 1824 John Dickens's mother died, leaving him £450. This was not a lot of money even back then, but it was enough to clear his debts and, on John Dickens's release from the Marshalsea prison, the family returned to Camden Town and lodged temporarily with Charles's landlady. It was during this time that John Dickens decided that his son should leave the factory and be placed in a school. Charles's mother, on the other hand, was quite satisfied that her son should remain where he was and an argument ensued which, though won by his father, meant that Dickens never quite forgave his mother for wishing such a meagre life for her son. In *Great Expectations* Pip remarks: 'In the little world in which children have their existence whosoever brings them up, there is nothing so finely perceived and so finely felt as injustice.' It can only be surmised that Dickens was remembering the injustice meted out to him by his mother. One thing is certain, however – like Pip, Dickens now set himself to triumph over his circumstances through sheer hard work.

Dickens attended Wellington House Academy – a mediocre establishment, where he stayed for two years, after which he became a clerk at the law firm of Ellis & Blackmore in Gray's Inn. During this time Dickens also began to visit the theatre regularly and persuaded several theatre managers to let him perform comic turns. Ever since he was a child and his father had set him up in taverns to sing and dance, it had been Dickens's wish to become an actor. Ironically he felt more himself when he was performing and his ability to mimic other people was legendary amongst his fellow workers. Dickens also thought, rightly or wrongly, that by becoming an actor he could leave, once and for all, the impoverished world he had come to inhabit and the meagre salary of a lawyer's clerk (approximately fifteen shillings per week), and establish himself with a modicum of wealth. Luckily for literature, Dickens's dreams of a life on the stage did not come to fruition. Instead, at the age of seventeen, he began scribbling down his observations on city life, on the people he met and came across in the street.

It was around this time that Dickens also determined to become a reporter for the political press and so enrolled on a shorthand course, which to everyone's amazement, he completed in just over three months (normally the course took three years to complete). Having learnt his trade he then went to work for *The Mirror of Parliament*. This was an exciting time to be a reporter. The Reform Bill was being made into law and there was a new Factory Act to control the number of hours that children should work, together with a new Poor Law. Charles threw himself into his job with gusto whilst at the same time contributing a series of stories to *Bell's Life in London* under the pen name 'Boz'. Then, at the age of twenty-three, Dickens was noticed by William Hall, a publisher with the company Chapman and Hall, who enquired whether he would be interested in writing a collection of stories about a group of Cockney sportsmen. The salary on offer was fourteen guineas a month.

This was a milestone in Dickens's writing career, for the collection would later become known as *The Pickwick Papers*, and following its success Dickens went on to write a serialization called *Oliver Twist* (1837–9), after which came *Nicholas Nickleby* (1838–9) and *The Old Curiosity Shop* (1840–1). All four of these novels, but in particular *Oliver Twist* and *Nicholas Nickleby* are vintage Dickens, displaying as they do, not only a social conscience, but also a concern for entertaining his audience. Indeed some of his most moving scenes are also some of his funniest and this flare for combining wit and wisdom was to become a trademark of all Dickens's best work.

Dickens was to publish fourteen major novels during his lifetime as well as numerous collections of short stories, plays and travel pieces, not to mention his many articles on social reform. He travelled, not only in Britain, but also to Europe and America, gave numerous readings of his work and vigorously campaigned on behalf of those less fortunate than himself. That his private life was no less frenetic is hardly surprising.

Having fallen in love and been rejected by a young woman called Maria Beadnell, Dickens went on in 1836 to marry Catherine Hogarth, the daughter of a fellow journalist, with whom he was to have ten children. It was during this marriage that Dickens wrote some of his most impressive work, namely *David Copperfield* (1849–50), which sold over 300,000 copies, *Bleak House* (1852–3), *Hard Times* (1854) and *Little Dorrit* (1855–7). Sadly however, Dickens's marriage was not to prove a happy one. Catherine was a shy, retiring woman who never really suited Dickens's outgoing temperament and, in 1858, much against Catherine's wishes, he separated from her and befriended a young actress called Ellen Ternan. There was at the time a great deal of conjecture about the nature of their relationship – whether she and Dickens were simply good friends, or whether they were lovers; and, indeed, speculations abounded as to whether or not she had given birth to Dickens's child (and if so whether or not that child had died) or had had an abortion. Whatever the case, Ellen Ternan became an important part of Dickens's life whereas Catherine did not, for, they separated and he went to live at Gad's Hill in Kent. It was here that he wrote *A Tale of Two Cities* (1859), *Great Expectations* (1860–1) and *Our Mutual Friend* (1863–4). However, by the mid-1860s Dickens's health was failing (most likely due to his heavy work schedule) and his last novel, *Edwin Drood* was sadly never completed.

On 8 June 1870, after a long day's work, Dickens suffered a stroke and he died the following day. Public grief was universal. He was buried in the Poets' Corner of Westminster Abbey, where his grave was laid open for two days during which time countless mourners came to pay their last respects.

The death of Charles Dickens marked the passing of an entire period for, just as we view Victorian England through his novels and the marvellous stories and characters he created, so the Victorians saw themselves through the writing of their most beloved artist.

Timeline of Charles Dickens's Life

1812 born in Portsmouth on 7 February, the second of eight children of John, a clerk in the Royal Navy Pay Office, and his wife Elizabeth

1821 spends the happiest period of his boyhood in Chatham, where his family moved in 1817. Charles is in this year sent to William Giles School

1823-4 starts work in a blacking factory, to his great humiliation, in order to help support his father's growing debts. Much of this miserable period in his life inspired parts of *David Copperfield*. Dickens's father, John, is imprisoned in Marshalsea debtors' prison for three months. On his release John removes his son from the factory and sends him back to school, this time at Wellington House Academy

1827 John Dickens again falls into debt, removing Charles from school. Charles then goes to work for a solicitor's, leaving after a year to become a freelance reporter

1828-35 reports on debates in the Commons for the

Morning Chronicle, much of what he saw informing works such as *Nicholas Nickleby* and *Bleak House*. Dickens also contributes to the *Monthly Magazine* (1833-5) and the *Evening Chronicle* (1835)

1836 his journalistic efforts lead to the serialization of his first novel, *The Pickwick Papers*. Marries Catherine Hogarth on 2 April, daughter of the *Evening Chronicle* editor

1837 birth of first of ten children, also named Charles. First serialization of *Oliver Twist* in *Bentley's Miscellany*. *Nicholas Nickleby* soon follows

1840 launches his new weekly, *Master Humphrey's Clock*, which carried *The Old Curiosity Shop* (1840-1) and *Barnaby Rudge* (1841)

1842 makes his first visit to America and Canada, where he is very well received, despite his advocating international copyright and the abolition of slavery

1843 writes *A Christmas Carol*, the first of a series of Christmas books, to meet the demands of the public and the further extension of his family with his wife's fifth pregnancy

1846 sets up Urania Cottage, a home for the reintegration of fallen women into society. About 100 women graduated between 1847 and 1859

1848–50 Dickens continues his success with the publication of *Dombey and Son* (1848) and *David Copperfield* (1849–50)

1852–7 publishes *Bleak House* (1852–3), *Hard Times* (1854), *Little Dorrit* (1855–7)

1857–8 Dickens co-writes and produces a fundraising performance of *The Frozen Deep* with Wilkie Collins and meets the actress Ellen Ternan. His immediate bond with her strains his already deteriorating relationship with his wife Catherine; they separate in 1858

1858 Dickens is asked by the founder of the Great Ormond Street Hospital to give a charitable speech to aid it in surviving a financial crisis. Dickens wholeheartedly complied, speaking at the hospital's first annual dinner and later giving a public reading of *A Christmas Carol* at St Martin-in-the-Fields church hall. His aid helped the hospital raise enough money to enable them to buy the neighbouring house and expand their number of beds from twenty to seventy-five

1858 embarks on a gruelling public reading tour of England, Scotland and Ireland, giving a total of eighty-seven performances

1859–61 *A Tale of Two Cities* (1859) and *Great Expectations* (1860-1) published. During this time he also published, edited and contributed to the journals of *Household Worlds* and *All the Year Round*

1865 survives the Staplehurst rail crash, where the first seven carriages fell off a bridge under repair. The only first-class carriage remaining was the one Dickens was in. He manages to retrieve the manuscript for *Our Mutual Friend*, which finished its publication run this year

1867–8 Dickens makes his second trip to America, spending four of his five months there giving public readings. It was on this trip that his health started to deteriorate; by the end of it he could barely manage solid foods

1868–9 gives a series of 'farewell readings' in England, Scotland and Ireland. After a mild stroke in April 1869, he later returns to make up the performances he missed due to his ill health

1870 makes his final public appearance at a Royal Academy Banquet in the presence of the Prince and Princess of Wales. He suffers another stroke on 8 June, and dies the following day at Gad's Hill Place in Higham, Kent, exactly five years after the Staplehurst crash. He is buried in the Poet's Corner of Westminster Abbey

His last novel, *The Mystery of Edwin Drood*, remained unfinished

Definition of a Horse: Childhood and Adolescence

Family life was at the centre of the Victorian social ideal but the period also nurtured some of the poorest living and working conditions for both children and adults, meaning family life was often far from pleasant. As if to make this point Dickens often populated his novels with highly dysfunctional families such as the Jellybys in *Bleak House* and the Gradgrinds in *Hard Times*, while several of his adult characters also testify to appalling experiences as waifs and strays having to fend for themselves. 'I've been locked up, as much as a silver tea-kettle . . .' says Magwitch in *Great Expectations*. 'I've been carted here and carted there, and put out of this town and put out of that town, and stuck in the stocks, and whipped and worried and drove. I've no more notion where I was born, than you have – if so much. I first become aware of myself, down in Essex, a-thieving turnips for my living. Summun had run away from me – a man – a tinker – and he'd took the fire with him, and left me wery cold.'

That Dickens suffered a similarly turbulent if not quite such a distressing time as a young boy is a matter of history and perhaps one that explains why the issue of childhood is so central to his work. But in addition to his fictional rampages,

Dickens also tried to be more constructive when it came to the poor, in particular by lobbying for a better educational system. Knowledge, Dickens instinctively felt, was the only way to improve children's lives and, as he was to write in the *Examiner*, 'Side by side with Crime, Disease, and Misery in England, Ignorance is always brooding, and is always certain to be found.'

Of course, most children ended up in factories such as the one Dickens himself worked in – a memory that pursued the writer throughout adult life to the extent that he sought to reform the whole system. For instance, having visited a factory at the bequest of the Earl of Shaftesbury, Dickens wrote, 'So far as seeing goes, I have seen enough for my purpose, and what I have seen has disgusted me and astonished me beyond all measure. I mean to strike the heaviest blow in my power for these unfortunate creatures . . .'

Today, some hundred and fifty years or so later, that 'heaviest blow' endures in Dickens's characters like the Artful Dodger, David Copperfield, Smike and Oliver Twist – that he could also extract a certain degree of humour when describing them, and the terrible situations they found themselves in, only attests to his immense skill as a writer.

Dombey sat in the corner of the darkened room in the great
armchair by the bedside, and Son lay tucked up warm in a little
basket bedstead, carefully disposed on a low settee immediately
in front of the fire and close to it, as if his constitution were
analogous to that of a muffin, and it was essential to toast him
brown while he was very new.
DOMBEY AND SON, 1846–8

'Well,' said my aunt, 'this is his boy – his son. He would be
as like his father as it's possible to be, if he was not so like
his mother, too.'
DAVID COPPERFIELD, 1849–50

Much vexed by this reflection, Mr Squeers looked at
the little boy to see whether he was doing anything he could
beat him for. As he happened not to be doing anything at all,
he merely boxed his ears, and told him
not to do it again.
NICHOLAS NICKLEBY, 1838–9

'Give me your definition of a horse.'
(Sissy Jupe thrown into the greatest alarm by this demand.)

'Girl number twenty unable to define a horse!' said Mr Gradgrind, for the general behoof of all the little pitchers. 'Girl number twenty possessed of no facts, in reference to one of the commonest of animals! Some boy's definition of a horse. Bitzer, yours.'

The square finger, moving here and there, lighted suddenly on Bitzer, perhaps because he chanced to sit in the same ray of sunlight which, darting in at one of the bare windows of the intensely whitewashed room, irradiated Sissy . . .

'Bitzer,' said Thomas Gradgrind. 'Your definition of a horse.'

'Quadruped. Graminivorous. Forty teeth, namely, twenty-four grinders, four eye-teeth, and twelve incisive. Sheds coat in the spring; in marshy countries, sheds hoofs, too. Hoofs hard, but requiring to be shod with iron. Age known by marks in mouth.' Thus (and much more) Bitzer.

'Now girl number twenty,' said Mr Gradgrind. 'You know what a horse is.'

HARD TIMES, 1854

The nephew revenges himself for this, by holding his breath and terrifying his kinswoman with the dread belief that he has made up his mind to burst. Regardless of whispers and shakes, he swells and becomes discoloured, and yet again swells and becomes discoloured, until the aunt can bear it no longer, but leads him out, with no visible neck, and with his eyes going before him like a prawn's.

'CITY OF LONDON CHURCHES',
THE UNCOMMERCIAL TRAVELLER, 1860

Some medical beast had revived tar-water in those days as a fine medicine, and Mrs Joe always kept a supply of it in the cupboard; having a belief in its virtues correspondent to its nastiness. At the best of times, so much of this elixir was administered to me as a choice restorative, that I was conscious of going about, smelling like a new fence.

PIP, *GREAT EXPECTATIONS*, 1860–1

'*My* mother? Bolted, ma'am!' said Bounderby. Mrs Gradgrind, stunned as usual, collapsed and gave it up. 'My mother left me to my grandmother,' said Bounderby; 'and, according to the best of my remembrance, my grandmother was the wickedest and the worst old woman that ever lived. If I got a little pair of shoes by any chance, she would take 'em off and sell 'em for drink. Why, I have known that grandmother of mine lie in her bed and drink her fourteen glasses of liquor before breakfast!'

Mrs Gradgrind, weakly smiling, and giving no other sign of vitality, looked (as she always did) like an indifferently executed transparency of a small female figure, without enough light behind it.

'She kept a chandler's shop,' pursued Bounderby, 'and kept me in an egg-box. That was the cot of *my* infancy; an old egg-box. As soon as I was big enough to run away, of course I ran away. Then I became a young vagabond; and instead of one old woman knocking me about and starving me, everybody of all ages knocked me about and starved me. They were right; they had no business to do anything else. I was a nuisance, an incumbrance, and a pest. I know that very well.'

HARD TIMES, 1854

'These, young ladies,' said Mrs Pardiggle, with great volubility, after the first salutations, 'are my five boys. You may have seen their names in a printed subscription list (perhaps more than one), in the possession of our esteemed friend Mr Jarndyce. Egbert, my eldest (twelve), is the boy who sent out his pocket-money, to the amount of five-and-threepence, to the Tockahoopo Indians. Oswald, my second (ten-and-a-half), is the child who contributed two-and-ninepence to the Great National Smithers Testimonial.

'Francis, my third (nine), one-and-sixpence-halfpenny; Felix, my fourth (seven), eightpence to the Superannuated Widows; Alfred, my youngest (five), has voluntarily enrolled himself in the Infant Bonds of Joy, and is pledged never, through life, to use tobacco in any form.'

We had never seen such dissatisfied children. It was not merely that they were weazened and shrivelled – though they were certainly that too – but they looked absolutely ferocious with discontent.

BLEAK HOUSE, 1852–3

I was always treated as if I had insisted on being born, in opposition to the dictates of reason, religion, and morality, and against the dissuading arguments of my best friends.
PIP, *GREAT EXPECTATIONS*, 1860–1

> It being a part of Mrs Pipchin's system not to
> encourage a child's mind to develop and expand
> itself like a young flower, but to open it by force
> like an oyster . . .
> *DOMBEY AND SON*, 1846–8

'We go upon the practical mode of teaching, Nickleby; the regular education system. C-l-e-a-n, clean, verb active, to make bright, to scour. W-i-n, win, d-e-r, der, winder, a casement. When the boy knows this out of book, he goes and does it. It's just the same principle as the use of globes. Where's the second boy?'

'Please, sir, he's weeding the garden,' replied a small voice.

'To be sure,' said Squeers, by no means disconcerted.

'So he is. B-o-t, bot, t-i-n, tin, bottin, n-e-y, ney, bottinney, noun substantive, a knowledge of plants. When he has learned that bottinney means a knowledge of plants, he goes and knows 'em. That's our system, Nickleby: what do you think of it?'

'It's a very useful one, at any rate,' answered Nicholas significantly.

'I believe you,' rejoined Squeers, not remarking the emphasis of his usher. 'Third boy, what's a horse?'

'A beast, sir,' replied the boy.

'So it is,' said Squeers. 'Ain't it, Nickleby?'

'I believe there is no doubt of that, sir,' answered Nicholas.

'Of course there isn't,' said Squeers. 'A horse is a quadruped, and quadruped's Latin for beast, as everybody that's gone through the grammar knows, or else where's the use of having grammars at all?'

'Where, indeed!' said Nicholas abstractedly.

'As you're perfect in that,' resumed Squeers, turning to the boy, 'go and look after *my* horse, and rub him down well, or I'll rub you down . . .'

NICHOLAS NICKLEBY, 1838–9

' . . . Now, here you see young David Copperfield, and the question I put to you is, what shall I do with him?'

'What shall you do with him?' said Mr Dick, feebly, scratching his head. 'Oh! do with him?'

'Yes,' said my aunt, with a grave look, and her forefinger held up. 'Come! I want some very sound advice.'

'Why, if I was you,' said Mr Dick, considering, and looking vacantly at me, 'I should – ' The contemplation of me seemed to inspire him with a sudden idea, and he added, briskly, 'I should wash him!'

'Janet,' said my aunt, turning round with a quiet triumph, which I did not then understand, 'Mr Dick sets us all right. Heat the bath!'

DAVID, DAVID COPPERFIELD, 1849–50

'Very well,' said this gentleman, briskly smiling, and folding his arms. 'That's a horse. Now, let me ask you girls and boys, Would you paper a room with representations of horses?'

After a pause, one half of the children cried in chorus, 'Yes, Sir!' Upon which the other half, seeing in the gentleman's face that Yes was wrong, cried out in chorus, 'No, Sir!' – as the custom is, in these examinations.

'Of course, No. Why wouldn't you?'

A pause. One corpulent slow boy, with a wheezy manner of breathing, ventured the answer, Because he wouldn't paper a room at all, but would paint it.

'You must paper it,' said the gentleman, rather warmly.

'You must paper it,' said Thomas Gradgrind, 'whether you like it or not. Don't tell us you wouldn't paper it. What do you mean, boy?'

'I'll explain to you, then,' said the gentleman, after another and a dismal pause, 'why you wouldn't paper a room with representations of horses. Do you ever see horses walking up and down the sides of rooms in reality – in fact? Do you?'

'Yes, Sir!' from one half. 'No, Sir!' from the other.

'Of course, No,' said the gentleman with an indignant look at the wrong half.

HARD TIMES, 1854

'The twins no longer derive their sustenance
from Nature's founts – in short,' said Mr
Micawber, in one of his bursts of confidence,
'they are weaned . . .'
DAVID COPPERFIELD, 1849–50

There Are
Strings:
Dickens in Love

D ickens first fell in love in 1829 when, at the age of seventeen, he met a young woman called Maria Beadnell. His affections were not reciprocated, in addition to which Maria's father, a banker, having discovered that Dickens's father had spent time in the Marshalsea, was against the match. Heartbroken, Dickens swore he would never fall in love again – but three years later he met and married Catherine Hogarth, with whom he had ten children. After they were married in 1836, rather than going to live by themselves, a third party joined them – Mary, Catherine's younger sister.

Mary was in awe of her brother-in-law and he of her. He constantly talked of her intelligence and beauty and at one point he describes her as 'so perfect a creature' as 'never breathed'. Tragically however, in May 1837, after returning from the theatre, Mary was suddenly taken ill (the doctors later said it was a heart attack) and died in Dickens's arms. Afterwards Dickens insisted on keeping all of Mary's clothes so that he could look at them when the whim took him, and he also said that he longed to be buried beside her. Mary came to represent an idealized picture of womanhood, one that Dickens used again and again in his novels when writing of virginal young girls, but most notably in the character of Little Nell in *The Old Curiosity Shop*.

Dickens remained with Catherine for twenty-two years – although the two were never ideally suited. In *David Copperfield*, his most autobiographical work, Dickens describes how the young David feels trapped by his wife . . . 'The old unhappy feeling', he writes, 'pervaded my life. It was deepened, if it were changed at all; but it was as undefined as ever, and addressed me like a strain of sorrowful music faintly heard in the night. I loved my wife dearly, and I was happy; but the happiness I had vaguely anticipated, once, was not the happiness I enjoyed, and there was always something wanting.'

That there was 'something wanting' in his own marriage was underlined only too clearly when, at the age of forty-six, Dickens met and fell in love with an eighteen-year-old actress called Ellen Ternan. In 1858 he and Catherine separated. Their separation was a bitter one with all sorts of allegations being made against Dickens, including one claim that he had committed incest with his sister-in-law, Georgina Hogarth (an allegation that was later proved unfounded). However, by that time the damage was done. 'My father', wrote Dickens's daughter, 'was like a madman . . . This affair brought out all that was worst – all that was weakest in him. He did not care a damn what happened to any of us.'

Finally Dickens secured his separation and he and Ellen Ternan continued seeing each other until the late 1860s when Dickens's health took a turn for the worse.

To say that Dickens was a romantic when it came to writing about love is an understatement as several of his novels prove, but as the following quotations attest, Dickens also had a wicked sense of humour concerning matters of the heart.

'. . . *we* know, Mr Weller – we, who are men of the world –
that a good uniform must work its way with the women,
sooner or later.'
'THE GENTLEMAN IN BLUE', *THE PICKWICK PAPERS*, 1846–7

Refused! refused by a teacher, picked up by
advertisement, at an annual salary of five pounds
payable at indefinite periods, and 'found' in food
and lodging like the very boys themselves . . .
NICHOLAS NICKLEBY, 1838–9

'The state of my feelings towards Miss Dombey is of that
unspeakable description, that my heart is a desert island, and
she lives in it alone. I'm getting more used up every day, and
I'm proud to be so. If you could see my legs when
I take my boots off, you'd form some idea of what
unrequited affection is.'
MR TOOTS, *DOMBEY AND SON*, 1846–8

'She's a very charming and delightful creature,' quoth Mr Robert Sawyer, in reply; 'and has only one fault that I know of, Ben. It happens, unfortunately, that that single blemish is a want of taste. She don't like me.'
THE PICKWICK PAPERS, 1846–7

Love, however, is very materially assisted by a warm and active imagination: which has a long memory, and will thrive, for a considerable time, on very slight and sparing food.
NICHOLAS NICKLEBY, 1838–9

It was understood that nothing of a tender nature could possibly be confided to old Barley, by reason of his being totally unequal to the consideration of any subject more psychological than gout, rum, and purser's stores.
GREAT EXPECTATIONS, 1860–1

D ombey and Son had often dealt in hides, but never in hearts. They left that fancy ware to boys and girls, and boarding-schools and books. Mr Dombey would have reasoned:

That a matrimonial alliance with himself *must*, in the nature of things, be gratifying and honourable to any woman of common sense. That the hope of giving birth to a new partner in such a house, could not fail to awaken a glorious and stirring ambition in the breast of the least ambitious of her sex.

DOMBEY AND SON, 1846–8

'And how, my sweet Miss Pecksniff,' said she [Mrs Todgers], 'how is your princely pa?'
Miss Pecksniff signified (in confidence) that he contemplated the introduction of a princely ma; and repeated the sentiment that she wasn't blind, and wasn't quite a fool, and wouldn't bear it.
MARTIN CHUZZLEWIT, 1843–4

There Are Strings

'There are strings,' said Mr Tappertit . . . 'in the
human heart that had better not be wibrated.'
SIMON TAPPERTIT, *BARNABY RUDGE*, 1841

I discovered afterwards that Miss Lavinia was an authority
in affairs of the heart, by reason of there having anciently
existed a certain Mr Pidger, who played short whist, and
was supposed to have been enamoured of her. My private
opinion is, that this was entirely a gratuitous assumption, and
that Pidger was altogether innocent of any such sentiments
– to which he had never given any sort of expression that
I could ever hear of. Both Miss Lavinia and Miss Clarissa
had a superstition, however, that he would have declared his
passion, if he had not been cut short in his youth (at about
sixty) by overdrinking his constitution, and over-doing an
attempt to set it right again by swilling Bath water.

DAVID, *DAVID COPPERFIELD*, 1849–50

'Oh, there's Ma being awful with somebody with a glass in his eye! Oh, I know she's going to bring him here! Oh, don't bring him, don't bring him! Oh, he'll be my partner with his glass in his eye! Oh, what shall I do?' This time Georgiana accompanied her ejaculations with taps of her feet upon the floor, and was altogether in quite a desperate condition. But, there was no escape from the majestic Mrs Podsnap's production of an ambling stranger, with one eye screwed up into extinction, and the other framed and glazed, who, having looked down out of that organ, as if he descried Miss Podsnap at the bottom of some perpendicular shaft, brought her to the surface, and ambled off with her.

OUR MUTUAL FRIEND, 1864–5

'Mrs Norton is perhaps the most beautiful, but the Duchess, to my mind, is the more kissable.'
OBSERVATION OF CHARLES DICKENS IN AMERICA, 1842

'Cows are my passion. What I have ever sighed
for, has been to retreat to a Swiss farm, and live
entirely surrounded by cows – and china.'
MRS SKEWTON, *DOMBEY AND SON*, 1846–8

On the seventh night of cribbage, when Mrs Todgers, sitting by, proposed that instead of gambling they should play for 'love', Mr Moddle was seen to change colour. On the fourteenth night, he kissed Miss Pecksniff's snuffers, in the passage, when she went upstairs to bed: meaning to have kissed her hand, but missing it.

In short, Mr Moddle began to be impressed with the idea that Miss Pecksniff's mission was to comfort him; and Miss Pecksniff began to speculate on the probability of its being her mission to become ultimately Mrs Moddle.

MARTIN CHUZZLEWIT, 1843–4

Bumblings

Amongst Dickens's host of lesser characters such as the Squeerses, the Pecksniffs, the Quilps, Heeps, Scrooges and Smallweeds, Mr Bumble, the workhouse beadle from *Oliver Twist*, is one of his most successful creations.

Dickens loathed petty officials; he hated their hypocrisy, their bigotry, their misplaced dogmatism and, most of all, the way they wielded power over those less fortunate than themselves. He was also very well acquainted with the iniquities of a society in which workhouses weren't so much places of safety as breeding grounds for malnutrition and disease (in 1839 nearly half the deaths in London were of children under the age of ten). All of these things were integrated by Dickens one way or another into *Oliver Twist* – indeed the scenes set in the workhouse were nothing less than a scathing indictment of the new Poor Law of 1834 – but with the character of Bumble, Dickens surpassed himself, using as he did caricature and burlesque to strengthen his arguments and give his comedy a bite seldom attempted before.

But, tears were not the things to find their way to Mr Bumble's soul; his heart was waterproof. Like washable beaver hats that improve with rain, his nerves were rendered stouter and more vigorous, by showers of tears, which, being tokens of weakness, and so far tacit admissions of his own power, pleased and exalted him. He eyed his good lady with looks of great satisfaction, and begged, in an encouraging manner, that she should cry her hardest: the exercise being looked upon, by the faculty, as strongly conducive to health.

'It opens the lungs, washes the countenance, exercises the eyes, and softens down the temper,' said Mr Bumble. 'So cry away.'

As he discharged himself of this pleasantry, Mr Bumble took his hat from a peg, and putting it on, rather rakishly, on one side, as a man might, who felt he had asserted his superiority in a becoming manner, thrust his hands into his pockets, and sauntered towards the door, with much ease and waggishness depicted in his whole appearance.

Now, Mrs Corney that was, had tried the tears, because they were less troublesome than a manual assault; but, she was quite prepared to make trial of the latter mode of proceeding, as Mr Bumble was not long in discovering.

The first proof he experienced of the fact, was conveyed in a hollow sound, immediately succeeded by the sudden flying off of his hat to the opposite end of the room. This preliminary proceeding laying bare his head, the expert lady, clasping him tightly round the throat with one hand, inflicted a shower of blows (dealt with singular vigour and dexterity) upon it with the other. This done, she created a little variety by scratching his face, and tearing his hair; and, having, by this time, inflicted as much punishment as she deemed necessary for the offence, she pushed him over a chair, which was luckily well situated for the purpose: and defied him to talk about his prerogative again, if he dared.

'Get up!' said Mrs Bumble, in a voice of command. 'And take yourself away from here, unless you want me to do something desperate.'

Mr Bumble rose with a very rueful countenance: wondering much what something desperate might be. Picking up his hat, he looked towards the door.

'Are you going?' demanded Mrs Bumble.

'Certainly, my dear, certainly,' rejoined Mr Bumble, making a quicker motion towards the door. 'I didn't intend to – I'm going, my dear! You are so very violent, that really I – '

At this instant, Mrs Bumble stepped hastily forward to replace the carpet, which had been kicked up in the scuffle. Mr Bumble immediately darted out of the room, without bestowing another thought on his unfinished sentence: leaving the late Mrs Corney in full possession of the field.

Mr Bumble was fairly taken by surprise, and fairly beaten. He had a decided propensity for bullying: derived no inconsiderable pleasure from the exercise of petty cruelty; and, consequently, was (it is needless to say) a coward. This is by no means a disparagement to his character; for many official personages, who are held in high respect and admiration, are the victims of similar infirmities. The remark is made, indeed, rather in his favour than otherwise, and with a view of impressing the reader with a just sense of his qualifications for office.

But, the measure of his degradation was not yet full. After making a tour of the house, and thinking, for the first time, that the poor-laws really were too hard on people; and that men who ran away from their wives, leaving them chargeable to the parish, ought, in justice, to be visited with no punishment at all, but rather rewarded as meritorious individuals who had suffered much; Mr Bumble came to a room where some of the female paupers were usually employed in washing the parish linen: whence the sound of voices in conversation, now proceeded.

'Hem!' said Mr Bumble, summoning up all his native dignity. 'These women at least shall continue to respect the prerogative. Hallo! hallo there! What do you mean by this noise, you hussies?'

With these words, Mr Bumble opened the door, and walked in with a very fierce and angry manner: which was at once exchanged for a most humiliated and cowering air, as his eyes unexpectedly rested on the form of his lady wife. 'My dear,' said Mr Bumble, 'I didn't know you were here.'

'Didn't know I was here!' repeated Mrs Bumble. 'What do YOU do here?'

'I thought they were talking rather too much to be doing

their work properly, my dear,' replied Mr Bumble: glancing distractedly at a couple of old women at the wash-tub, who were comparing notes of admiration at the workhouse-master's humility.

'YOU thought they were talking too much?' said Mrs Bumble. 'What business is it of yours?'

'Why, my dear – ' urged Mr Bumble submissively.

'What business is it of yours?' demanded Mrs Bumble, again.

'It's very true, you're matron here, my dear,' submitted Mr Bumble; 'but I thought you mightn't be in the way just then.'

'I'll tell you what, Mr Bumble,' returned his lady. 'We don't want any of your interference. You're a great deal too fond of poking your nose into things that don't concern you, making everybody in the house laugh, the moment your back is turned, and making yourself look like a fool every hour in the day. Be off; come!'

Mr Bumble, seeing with excruciating feelings, the delight of the two old paupers, who were tittering together most rapturously, hesitated for an instant. Mrs Bumble, whose patience brooked no delay, caught up a bowl of soap-suds, and motioning him towards the door, ordered him instantly to depart, on pain of receiving the contents upon his portly person. What could Mr Bumble do? He looked dejectedly round, and slunk away; and, as he reached the door, the titterings of the paupers broke into a shrill chuckle of irrepressible delight. It wanted but this. He was degraded in their eyes; he had lost caste and station before the very paupers; he had fallen from all the height and pomp of beadleship, to the lowest depth of the most snubbed henpeckery.

'All in two months!' said Mr Bumble, filled with dismal thoughts. 'Two months! No more than two months ago, I was not only my own master, but everybody else's, so far as the porochial workhouse was concerned, and now! —'

OLIVER TWIST, 1837–9

He Had But One Eye: Dickens's Characters

Of all the outstanding features of a Dickens novel or short story, it is the vast array of characters that remain in the reader's mind long after finishing the book. In fact, with the exception of Shakespeare, I can think of no other author whose characters are part and parcel of the national consciousness as those of Charles Dickens. Think of Mr Micawber or Fagin, or Magwitch, not to mention Oliver Twist, David Copperfield or Scrooge. Characters and their small foibles were Dickens's meat and potatoes but, as he remarked on several occasions, none lived in his imagination until he had found them a name and so whenever he spied an interesting one (from a register perhaps, or from a gravestone) he would always take care to scribble it down in a notebook.

More than that, Dickens created characters by letting them evolve in his imagination. 'Suppose,' he once said to a group of friends, picking up a glass, 'Suppose I choose to call this a *character*, fancy it a man, endue it with certain qualities; and soon the fine filmy webs of thought, almost impalpable, coming from every direction, we know not whence, spin and weave about it, until it achieves form and beauty, and becomes instinct with life.' This process Dickens called the 'unfathomable mystery', but it must be due in part not only to the visual richness of his descriptions but also to his comic genius for summing people up as much through their faults as through anything else.

Mr Squeers's appearance was not prepossessing. He had but one eye, and the popular prejudice runs in favour of two.
NICHOLAS NICKLEBY, 1838–9

Mrs Joe was a very clean housekeeper, but had an exquisite art of making her cleanliness more uncomfortable and unacceptable than dirt itself.
GREAT EXPECTATIONS, 1860–1

The man who now confronted Gashford, was a squat, thickset personage, with a low, retreating forehead, a coarse shock head of hair, and eyes so small and near together, that his broken nose alone seemed to prevent their meeting and fusing into one of the usual size.
BARNABY RUDGE, 1841

Mr Podsnap was well-to-do, and stood very high in Mr Podsnap's opinion.
OUR MUTUAL FRIEND, 1864–5

. . . I had a latent impression that there was something decidedly fine in Mr Wopsle's elocution – not for old association's sake, I am afraid, but because it was very slow, very dreary, very up-hill and down-hill, and very unlike any way in which any man in any natural circumstances of life or death ever expressed himself about anything.

PIP, *GREAT EXPECTATIONS*, 1860–1

Mr Barnacle dated from a better time, when the country was not so parsimonious, and the Circumlocution Office was not so badgered. He wound and wound folds of white cravat round his neck, as he wound and wound folds of tape and paper round the neck of the country.

LITTLE DORRIT, 1855–7

Mr Chadband is a large yellow man, with a fat smile, and a general appearance of having a good deal of train oil in his system.

BLEAK HOUSE, 1852–3

Mr Sparkler, stimulated by Love to brilliancy, replied that for a particular walk, a man ought to have a particular pair of shoes: as, for example, shooting, shooting-shoes; cricket, cricket-shoes. Whereas, he believed that Henry Gowan had no particular pair of shoes.

'No speciality?' said Mr Dorrit.

This being a very long word for Mr Sparkler, and his mind being exhausted by his late effort, he replied, 'No, thank you. I seldom take it.'

LITTLE DORRIT, 1855–7

Most public characters have their failings; and the truth is that Mr Snevellicci was a little addicted to drinking; or, if the whole truth must be told, that he was scarcely ever sober. He knew in his cups three distinct stages of intoxication,– the dignified – the quarrelsome – the amorous. When professionally engaged he never got beyond the dignified; in private circles he went through all three, passing from one to another with a rapidity of transition often rather perplexing to those who had not the honour of his acquaintance.

NICHOLAS NICKLEBY, 1838–9

'Any man may be in good spirits and good temper when he's well dressed. There ain't much credit in that.'
MARK TAPLEY, *MARTIN CHUZZLEWIT*, 1843–4

Sooth to say, he was so wooden a man that he seemed to have taken his wooden leg naturally, and rather suggested to the fanciful observer that he might be expected – if his development received no untimely check – to be completely set up with a pair of wooden legs in about six months.
OUR MUTUAL FRIEND, 1864–5, OF SILAS WEGG

'That's a woman who observes and reflects in an uncommon manner. She's the sort of woman now,' said Mould, drawing his silk handkerchief over his head again, and composing himself for a nap 'one would almost feel disposed to bury for nothing: and do it neatly, too!'
MARTIN CHUZZLEWIT, 1843–4, OF SARAH GAMP

Regarded as a classical ruin, Mrs Sparsit was an interesting spectacle on her arrival at her journey's end; but considered in any other light, the amount of damage she had by that time sustained was excessive, and impaired her claims to admiration.
HARD TIMES, 1854

'Dumb as a drum vith a hole in it, sir.'
SAM WELLER, *THE PICKWICK PAPERS*, 1836–7

In his lifetime, and likewise in the period of Snagsby's 'time' of seven long years, there dwelt with Peffer, in the same law-stationering premises, a niece – a short, shrewd niece, something too violently compressed about the waist, and with a sharp nose like a sharp autumn evening, inclining to be frosty towards the end.
BLEAK HOUSE, 1852–3

'Annual income twenty pounds, annual expenditure nineteen nineteen six, result happiness. Annual income twenty pounds, annual expenditure twenty pounds ought and six, result misery. The blossom is blighted, the leaf is withered, the God of day goes down upon the dreary scene, and – and in short you are for ever floored. As I am!'
MR MICAWBER, *DAVID COPPERFIELD*, 1849–50

'Warm weather, Mrs Lammle,' said Fascination Fledgeby. Mrs Lammle thought it scarcely as warm as it had been yesterday. 'Perhaps not,' said Fascination Fledgeby with great quickness of repartee; 'but I expect it will be devilish warm to-morrow.'
OUR MUTUAL FRIEND, 1864–5

'Blood cannot be obtained from a stone, neither can anything on account be obtained at present (not to mention law expenses) from Mr Micawber.'
MRS MICAWBER, *DAVID COPPERFIELD*, 1849–50

Why, Mr Bounderby was as near being Mr Gradgrind's bosom friend, as a man perfectly devoid of sentiment can approach that spiritual relationship towards another man perfectly devoid of sentiment. So near was Mr Bounderby – or, if the reader should prefer it, so far off.

He was a rich man: banker, merchant, manufacturer, and what not. A big, loud man, with a stare, and a metallic laugh. A man made out of a coarse material, which seemed to have been stretched to make so much of him. A man with a great puffed head and forehead, swelled veins in his temples, and such a strained skin to his face that it seemed to hold his eyes open, and lift his eyebrows up. A man with a pervading appearance on him of being inflated like a balloon, and ready to start. A man who could never sufficiently vaunt himself a self-made man. A man who was always proclaiming, through that brassy speaking trumpet of a voice of his, his old ignorance and his old poverty. A man who was the Bully of humility.

A year or two younger than his eminently practical friend, Mr Bounderby looked older; his seven or eight and forty might have had the seven or eight added to it again, without surprising anybody. He had not much hair. One might have fancied he had talked it off; and that what was left, all standing up in disorder, was in that condition from being constantly blown about by his windy boastfulness.

HARD TIMES, 1854

Mrs Varden was disposed to be amazingly cheerful. Indeed the worthy housewife was of such a capricious nature, that she not only attained a higher pitch of genius than Macbeth, in respect of her ability to be wise, amazed, temperate and furious, loyal and neutral in an instant, but would sometimes ring the changes backwards and forwards on all possible moods and flights in one short quarter of an hour; performing, as it were, a kind of triple bob major on the peal of instruments in the female belfry, with a skilfulness and rapidity of execution that astonished all who heard her.

BARNABY RUDGE, 1841

'Ah! . . . he'd make a lovely corpse.'
SARAH GAMP, *MARTIN CHUZZLEWIT*, 1843–4,
OF A PATIENT

The Podsnaps lived in a shady angle adjoining Portman Square. They were a kind of people certain to dwell in the shade, wherever they dwelt.

OUR MUTUAL FRIEND, 1864–5

First, there was Mr Spottletoe, who was so bald and had
such big whiskers, that he seemed to have stopped his hair,
by the sudden application of some powerful remedy, in
the very act of falling off his head, and to have fastened it
irrevocably on his face.
MARTIN CHUZZLEWIT, 1843–4

Notwithstanding his very liberal laudation of himself, however,
the Major was selfish. It may be doubted whether there ever
was a more entirely selfish person at heart; or at stomach is
perhaps a better expression, seeing that he was more decidedly
endowed with that latter organ than with the former.
DOMBEY AND SON, 1846–8

Of an ungainly make was Sloppy. Too much of him
longwise, too little of him broad wise, and too many sharp
angles of him angle-wise. One of those shambling male
human creatures, born to be indiscreetly candid in the
revelation of buttons . . .
OUR MUTUAL FRIEND, 1864–5

She was a fat old woman, this Mrs Gamp, with a husky voice and a moist eye, which she had a remarkable power of turning up, and only showing the white of it. Having very little neck, it cost her some trouble to look over herself, if one may say so, at those to whom she talked. . . . The face of Mrs Gamp – the nose in particular – was somewhat red and swollen, and it was difficult to enjoy her society without becoming conscious of a smell of spirits.
MARTIN CHUZZLEWIT, 1843–4

'I needn't beg you,' [Mr Dombey] added, pausing for a moment at the settee before the fire, 'to take particular care of this young gentleman, Mrs . . .'
'Blockitt, Sir?' suggested the nurse, a simpering piece of faded gentility, who did not presume to state her name as a fact, but merely offered it as a mild suggestion.
DOMBEY AND SON, 1846–8

He Had But One Eye

Sim, as he was called in the locksmith's family, or Mr Simon Tappertit, as he called himself, and required all men to style him out of doors, on holidays, and Sundays out, – was an old-fashioned, thin-faced, sleek-haired, sharp-nosed, small-eyed little fellow, very little more than five feet high, and thoroughly convinced in his own mind that he was above the middle size; rather tall, in fact, than otherwise. Of his figure, which was well enough formed, though somewhat of the leanest, he entertained the highest admiration; and with his legs, which, in knee-breeches, were perfect curiosities of littleness, he was enraptured to a degree amounting to enthusiasm. He also had some majestic, shadowy ideas, which had never been quite fathomed by his intimate friends, concerning the power of his eye. Indeed he had been known to go so far as to boast that he could utterly quell and subdue the haughtiest beauty by a simple process, which he termed 'eyeing her over'; but it must be added, that neither of this faculty, nor of the power he claimed to have, through the same gift, of vanquishing and heaving down dumb animals, even in a rabid state, had he ever furnished evidence which could be deemed quite satisfactory and conclusive.

BARNABY RUDGE, 1841

Sir Leicester Dedlock is only a baronet, but there is no mightier baronet than he. His family is as old as the hills, and infinitely more respectable. He has a general opinion that the world might get on without hills, but would be done up without Dedlocks.

BLEAK HOUSE, 1852–3

Now, Mr Bumble was a fat man, and a choleric; so, instead of responding to this open-hearted salutation in a kindred spirit, he gave the little wicket a tremendous shake, and then bestowed upon it a kick which could have emanated from no leg but a beadle's.

OLIVER TWIST, 1837–9

Of his architectural doings, nothing was clearly known, except that he had never designed or built anything; but it was generally understood that his knowledge of the science was almost awful in its profundity.

MARTIN CHUZZLEWIT, 1843–4, OF MR PECKSNIFF

Mrs Micawber was quite as elastic. I have known her to be thrown into fainting fits by the King's taxes at three o'clock, and to eat lamb-chops, breaded, and drink warm ale (paid for with two teaspoons that had gone to the pawnbroker's) at four.

DAVID, *DAVID COPPERFIELD*, 1849–50

M^r and Mrs Veneering were brand-new people in a brand-new house in a brand-new quarter in London. Everything about the Veneerings was spick-and-span new. All their furniture was new, all their friends were new, all their servants were new, their plate was new, their carriage was new, their harness was new, their horses were new, their pictures were new, they themselves were new, they were as newly married as was lawfully compatible with their having a brand-new baby, and, if they had set up a great-grandfather, he would have come home in matting from the Pantechnicon, without a scratch upon him, French polished to the crown of his head.

OUR MUTUAL FRIEND, 1864–5

. . . although a skilful flatterer is a most delightful companion, if you can keep him all to yourself, his taste becomes very doubtful when he takes to complimenting other people.

NICHOLAS NICKLEBY, 1838–9

Mrs Varden was a lady of what is commonly called an uncertain temper – a phrase which being interpreted signifies a temper tolerably certain to make everybody more or less uncomfortable.

BARNABY RUDGE, 1841

'Peggotty!' repeated Miss Betsey, with some indignation. 'Do you mean to say, child, that any human being has gone into a Christian church, and got herself named Peggotty?'

DAVID COPPERFIELD, 1849–50

'You are a pair of Whittingtons, gents, without the cat; which is a most agreeable and blessed exception to me, for I am not attached to the feline species. My name is Tigg; how do you do?'
TIGG MONTAGUE, *MARTIN CHUZZLEWIT*, 1843–4

It was not a bosom to repose upon, but it was a capital bosom to hang jewels upon.
LITTLE DORRIT, 1855–7, OF MRS MERDLE

One might infer, from Judy's appearance, that her business rather lay with the thorns than the flowers . . .
BLEAK HOUSE, 1852–3

Demmit!

In his long career as both a novelist and playwright Charles Dickens created many wonderful characters, but none tickle the fancy in quite the same fashion as Mr Mantalini from *Nicholas Nickleby*.

Written shortly after *Oliver Twist, Nicholas Nickleby*, as well as being a searing indictment of the 'Yorkshire schools' (institutions largely used for the dumping of illegitimate children), is also a comic masterpiece, containing such notable figures as the theatrical Mr and Mrs Crummles, alongside their daughter the 'Infant Phenomenon', Mrs Wititterly who spends much of her time reclining on a sofa and last, but certainly not least, Mrs Nickleby, who can never quite remember what she is talking about. Some people also regard the grotesque Squeers family as being comic and, in their way, they are (in particular poor Fanny Squeers). And, last but certainly not least, there is Mr Mantalini, whose improbable endearments towards his long-suffering wife, such as calling her his 'essential juice of pineapple', are second to none and read as freshly today as they must have done in Dickens's time.

'Let me see the names,' replied Ralph, impatiently extending his hand for the bills. 'Well! They are not sure, but they are safe enough. Do you consent to the terms, and will you take the money? I don't want you to do so. I would rather you didn't.'

'Demmit, Nickleby, can't you –' began Mr Mantalini.

'No,' replied Ralph, interrupting him. 'I can't. Will you take the money – down, mind; no delay, no going into the City and pretending to negotiate with some other party who has no existence, and never had. Is it a bargain, or is it not?'

Ralph pushed some papers from him as he spoke, and carelessly rattled his cash-box, as though by mere accident. The sound was too much for Mr Mantalini. He closed the bargain directly it reached his ears, and Ralph told the money out upon the table.

He had scarcely done so, and Mr Mantalini had not yet gathered it all up, when a ring was heard at the bell, and immediately afterwards Newman ushered in no less a person than Madame Mantalini, at sight of whom Mr Mantalini evinced considerable discomposure, and swept the cash into his pocket with remarkable alacrity.

'Oh, you *are* here,' said Madame Mantalini, tossing her head.

'Yes, my life and soul, I am,' replied her husband, dropping on his knees, and pouncing with kitten-like playfulness upon a stray sovereign. 'I am here, my soul's delight, upon Tom Tiddler's ground, picking up the demnition gold and silver.'

'I am ashamed of you,' said Madame Mantalini, with much indignation.

'Ashamed – of *me*, my joy? It knows it is talking demd charming sweetness, but naughty fibs,' returned Mr Mantalini. 'It knows it is not ashamed of its own popolorum tibby.'

Whatever were the circumstances which had led to such a result, it certainly appeared as though the popolorum tibby had rather miscalculated, for the nonce, the extent of his lady's affection. Madame Mantalini only looked scornful in reply; and, turning to Ralph, begged him to excuse her intrusion.

'Which is entirely attributable,' said Madame, 'to the gross misconduct and most improper behaviour of Mr Mantalini.'

'Of me, my essential juice of pineapple!'

'Of you,' returned his wife. 'But I will not allow it. I will not submit to be ruined by the extravagance and profligacy of any man. I call Mr Nickleby to witness the course I intend to pursue with you.'

'Pray don't call me to witness anything, ma'am,' said Ralph. 'Settle it between yourselves, settle it between yourselves.'

'No, but I must beg you as a favour,' said Madame Mantalini, 'to hear me give him notice of what it is my fixed intention to do – my fixed intention, sir,' repeated Madame Mantalini, darting an angry look at her husband.

'Will she call me "Sir"?' cried Mantalini. 'Me who dote upon her with the demdest ardour! She, who coils her fascinations round me like a pure angelic rattlesnake! It will be all up with my feelings; she will throw me into a demd state.'

'Don't talk of feelings, sir,' rejoined Madame Mantalini, seating herself, and turning her back upon him. 'You don't consider mine.'

'I do not consider yours, my soul!' exclaimed Mr Mantalini.

'No,' replied his wife.

And notwithstanding various blandishments on the part of Mr Mantalini, Madame Mantalini still said no, and said it too with such determined and resolute ill-temper, that Mr Mantalini was clearly taken aback.

'His extravagance, Mr Nickleby,' said Madame Mantalini, addressing herself to Ralph, who leant against his easy-chair with his hands behind him, and regarded the amiable couple with a smile of the supremest and most unmitigated contempt, – 'his extravagance is beyond all bounds.'

'I should scarcely have supposed it,' answered Ralph, sarcastically.

'I assure you, Mr Nickleby, however, that it is,' returned Madame Mantalini. 'It makes me miserable! I am under constant apprehensions, and in constant difficulty. And even this,' said Madame Mantalini, wiping her eyes, 'is not the worst. He took some papers of value out of my desk this morning without asking my permission.'

Mr Mantalini groaned slightly, and buttoned his trousers pocket.

'I am obliged,' continued Madame Mantalini, 'since our late misfortunes, to pay Miss Knag a great deal of money for having her name in the business, and I really cannot afford to encourage him in all his wastefulness. As I have no doubt that he came straight here, Mr Nickleby, to convert the papers I have spoken of, into money, and as you have assisted us very often before, and are very much connected with us in this kind of matters, I wish you to know the determination at which his conduct has compelled me to arrive.'

Mr Mantalini groaned once more from behind his wife's bonnet, and fitting a sovereign into one of his eyes, winked with the other at Ralph. Having achieved this performance with great dexterity, he whipped the coin into his pocket, and groaned again with increased penitence.

'I have made up my mind,' said Madame Mantalini, as tokens of impatience manifested themselves in Ralph's countenance, 'to allowance him.'

'To do that, my joy?' inquired Mr Mantalini, who did not seem to have caught the words.

'To put him,' said Madame Mantalini, looking at Ralph, and prudently abstaining from the slightest glance at her husband, lest his many graces should induce her to falter in her resolution, 'to put him upon a fixed allowance; and I say that if he has a hundred and twenty pounds a year for his clothes and pocket-money, he may consider himself a very fortunate man.'

Mr Mantalini waited, with much decorum, to hear the amount of the proposed stipend, but when it reached his ears, he cast his hat and cane upon the floor, and drawing out his pocket-handkerchief, gave vent to his feelings in a dismal moan.

'Demnition!' cried Mr Mantalini, suddenly skipping out of his chair, and as suddenly skipping into it again, to the great discomposure of his lady's nerves. 'But no. It is a demd horrid dream. It is not reality. No!'

Comforting himself with this assurance, Mr Mantalini closed his eyes and waited patiently till such time as he should wake up.

'A very judicious arrangement,' observed Ralph with a sneer, 'if your husband will keep within it, ma'am – as no doubt he will.'

'Demmit!' exclaimed Mr Mantalini, opening his eyes at the sound of Ralph's voice, 'it is a horrid reality. She is sitting there before me. There is the graceful outline of her form; it cannot be mistaken – there is nothing like it. The two countesses had no outlines at all, and the dowager's was a demd outline. Why is she so excruciatingly beautiful that I cannot be angry with her, even now?'

'You have brought it upon yourself, Alfred,' returned Madame Mantalini – still reproachfully, but in a softened tone.

'I am a demd villain!' cried Mr Mantalini, smiting himself on the head. 'I will fill my pockets with change for a sovereign in halfpence and drown myself in the Thames; but I will not be angry with her, even then, for I will put a note in the twopenny-post as I go along, to tell her where the body is.

She will be a lovely widow. I shall be a body. Some handsome women will cry; she will laugh demnebly.'

'Alfred, you cruel, cruel creature,' said Madame Mantalini, sobbing at the dreadful picture.

'She calls me cruel – me – me – who for her sake will become a demd, damp, moist, unpleasant body!' exclaimed Mr Mantalini.

'You know it almost breaks my heart, even to hear you talk of such a thing,' replied Madame Mantalini.

'Can I live to be mistrusted?' cried her husband. 'Have I cut my heart into a demd extraordinary number of little pieces, and given them all away, one after another, to the same little engrossing demnition captivator, and can I live to be suspected by her? Demmit, no I can't.'

'Ask Mr Nickleby whether the sum I have mentioned is not a proper one,' reasoned Madame Mantalini.

'I don't want any sum,' replied her disconsolate husband; 'I shall require no demd allowance. I will be a body.'

On this repetition of Mr Mantalini's fatal threat, Madame Mantalini wrung her hands, and implored the interference of Ralph Nickleby; and after a great quantity of tears and talking, and several attempts on the part of Mr Mantalini to reach the door, preparatory to straightway committing violence upon himself, that gentleman was prevailed upon, with difficulty, to promise that he wouldn't be a body. This great point attained, Madame Mantalini argued the question of the allowance, and Mr Mantalini did the same, taking occasion to show that he could live with uncommon satisfaction upon bread and water, and go clad in rags, but that he could not support existence with the additional burden of being mistrusted by the object of his most devoted and disinterested affection. This brought fresh tears into Madame Mantalini's eyes, which having just begun to open to some few of the demerits of Mr Mantalini, were only open a very little way, and could be easily closed again. The result was, that without quite giving up the allowance question, Madame Mantalini postponed its further consideration; and Ralph saw, clearly enough, that Mr Mantalini had gained a fresh lease of his easy life, and that, for some time longer at all events, his degradation and downfall were postponed.

NICHOLAS NICKLEBY, 1838–9

I Am Miserable: Husbands and Wives

That Dickens's own marriage to Catherine Hogarth was not an entirely happy one is a well-documented fact. However, they *did* spend twenty-two years together and they *did* have ten children, so it is not unlikely that they enjoyed some happiness during this time. That being said, Catherine and Charles were not equally matched – indeed at one point Dickens wrote to his friend (and later his biographer) John Forster:

> Poor Catherine and I are not made for each other, and there is no help for it. It is not only that she makes me uneasy and unhappy, but that I make her so too – and much more so. She is exactly what you know, in the way of being amiable and complying; but we are strangely ill-assorted for the bond there is between us. God knows she would have been a thousand times happier if she had married another kind of man, and that her avoidance of this destiny would have been at least equally good for us both.

Other pressures on their partnership no doubt included the fact that over the course of their marriage Dickens turned from being an unknown writer into one of the most adored and famous men in the country, as well as the fact that two of Catherine's sisters (Mary and Georgina) came to live with them and, over a period of time, strongly endeared themselves to her husband.

Of his fictional partnerships, Mr and Mrs Lammle are perhaps the saddest and most sinister whereas Mr and Madame Mantalini emerge as the funniest. On the other hand Mr and Mrs Bumble run the Mantalinis a close second and Mr and Mrs Crummles, though not at each other's throats, make a splendidly humorous pair.

'I've found a sov'rin' cure for that, Sammy,' said Mr Weller, setting down the glass.

'A sovereign cure for the gout,' said Mr Pickwick hastily producing his note-book. 'What is it?'

'The gout, sir,' replied Mr Weller, 'the gout is a complaint as arises from too much ease and comfort. If ever you're attacked with the gout, sir, jist you marry a wider as has got a good loud voice, with a decent notion of usin' it, and you'll never have the gout agin.'

THE PICKWICK PAPERS, 1836–7

'It runs in the family, I b'lieve, sir,' replied Mr Weller. 'My father's wery much in that line now. If my mother-in-law blows him up, he whistles. She flies in a passion and breaks his pipe; he steps out and gets another. Then she screams wery loud and falls into 'sterics; and he smokes wery comfortably till she comes to agin. That's philosophy, sir, ain't it?'

THE PICKWICK PAPERS, 1836–7

Beside him is a spare cushion, with which he is always provided, in order that he may have something to throw at the venerable partner of his respected age whenever she makes an allusion to money – a subject on which he is particularly sensitive.

'And where's Bart?' Grandfather Smallweed inquires of Judy, Bart's twin-sister.

'He ain't come in yet,' says Judy.

'It's his tea-time, isn't it?'

'No.'

'How much do you mean to say it wants then?'

'Ten minutes.'

'Hey?'

'Ten minutes.' (Loud on the part of Judy.)

'Ho!' says Grandfather Smallweed. 'Ten minutes.'

Grandmother Smallweed, who has been mumbling and shaking her head at the trivets, hearing figures mentioned, connects them with money, and screeches, like a horrible old parrot without any plumage, 'Ten, ten-pound notes!'

Grandfather Smallweed immediately throws the cushion at her.

'Drat you, be quiet!' says the good old man.

BLEAK HOUSE, 1852–3

'Are you going to sit snoring there, all day?' inquired Mrs Bumble.

'I am going to sit here, as long as I think proper, ma'am,' rejoined Mr Bumble; 'and although I was *not* snoring, I shall snore, gape, sneeze, laugh, or cry, as the humour strikes me; such being my prerogative.'

'*Your* prerogative!' sneered Mrs Bumble, with ineffable contempt.

'I said the word, ma'am,' said Mr Bumble. 'The prerogative of a man is to command.'

'And what's the prerogative of a woman, in the name of Goodness?' cried the relict of Mr Corney deceased.

'To obey, ma'am,' thundered Mr Bumble.

OLIVER TWIST, 1837–9

Mr and Mrs Lammle have walked for some time on the Shanklin sands, and one may see by their footprints that they have not walked arm in arm, and that they have not walked in a straight track, and that they have walked in a moody humour; for, the lady has prodded little spurting holes in the damp sand before her with her parasol, and the gentleman has trailed his stick after him. As if he were of the Mephistopheles family indeed, and had walked with a drooping tail.

OUR MUTUAL FRIEND, 1864–5

In this attitude he fell directly into a reverie, from which he was only aroused by his wife's calling to him from her ottoman, when they had been for some quarter-of-an-hour alone.

'Eh? Yes?' said Mr Merdle, turning towards her. 'What is it?'

'What is it?' repeated Mrs Merdle. 'It is, I suppose, that you have not heard a word of my complaint.'

'Your complaint, Mrs Merdle?' said Mr Merdle. 'I didn't know that you were suffering from a complaint. What complaint?'

'A complaint of you,' said Mrs Merdle.

'Oh! A complaint of me,' said Mr Merdle. 'What is the – what have I – what may you have to complain of in me, Mrs Merdle?'

In his withdrawing, abstracted, pondering way, it took him some time to shape this question. As a kind of faint attempt to convince himself that he was the master of the house, he concluded by presenting his forefinger to the parrot, who expressed his opinion on that subject by instantly driving his bill into it.

'You were saying, Mrs Merdle,' said Mr Merdle, with his wounded finger in his mouth, 'that you had a complaint against me?'

'A complaint which I could scarcely show the justice of more emphatically, than by having to repeat it,' said Mrs Merdle. 'I might as well have stated it to the wall. I had far better have stated it to the bird. He would at least have screamed.'

LITTLE DORRIT, 1855–7

There was, however, the sound of voices in conversation in the next room; and as the conversation was loud and the partition thin, Kate could not help discovering that they belonged to Mr and Mrs Mantalini.

'If you will be odiously, demnebly, outrigeously jealous, my soul,' said Mr Mantalini, 'you will be very miserable – horrid miserable – demnition miserable.' And then, there came a sound as though Mr Mantalini were sipping his coffee.

'I am miserable,' returned Madame Mantalini, evidently pouting.

'Then you are an ungrateful, unworthy, demd unthankful little fairy,' said Mr Mantalini.

'I am not,' returned Madame, with a sob.

'Do not put itself out of humour,' said Mr Mantalini, breaking an egg. 'It is a pretty bewitching little demd countenance, and it should not be out of humour, for it spoils its loveliness, and makes it cross and gloomy like a frightful, naughty, demd hobgoblin.'

'I am not to be brought round in that way, always,' rejoined Madame, sulkily.

'It shall be brought round in any way it likes best, and not brought round at all if it likes that better,' retorted Mr Mantalini, with his egg-spoon in his mouth.

'It's very easy to talk,' said Mrs Mantalini.

'Not so easy when one is eating a demnition egg,' replied Mr Mantalini; 'for the yolk runs down the waistcoat, and yolk of egg does not match any waistcoat but a yellow waistcoat, demmit.'

'You were flirting with her during the whole night,' said Madame Mantalini, apparently desirous to lead the conversation back to the point from which it had strayed.

'No, no, my life.'

'You were,' said Madame; 'I had my eye upon you all the time.'

'Bless the little winking twinkling eye; was it on me all the time!' cried Mantalini, in a sort of lazy rapture. 'Oh, demmit!'

'And I say once more,' resumed Madame, 'that you ought not to waltz with anybody but your own wife; and I will not bear it, Mantalini, if I take poison first.'

'She will not take poison and have horrid pains, will she?' said Mantalini; who, by the altered sound of his voice, seemed to have moved his chair and taken up his position nearer to his wife. 'She will not take poison, because she had a demd fine husband who might have married two countesses and a dowager –'

'Two countesses,' interposed Madame. 'You told me one before!'

'Two!' cried Mantalini. 'Two demd fine women, real countesses and splendid fortunes, demmit.'

'And why didn't you?' asked Madame, playfully.

'Why didn't I!' replied her husband. 'Had I not seen, at a morning concert, the demdest little fascinator in all the world, and while that little fascinator is my wife, may not all the countesses and dowagers in England be –'

Mr Mantalini did not finish the sentence, but he gave Madame Mantalini a very loud kiss, which Madame Mantalini returned; after which, there seemed to be some more kissing mixed up with the progress of the breakfast.

NICHOLAS NICKLEBY, 1838–9

'...Look at her – mother of six children – three of 'em alive, and all upon the stage!'

'Extraordinary!' cried Nicholas.

'Ah! extraordinary indeed,' rejoined Mr Crummles, taking a complacent pinch of snuff, and shaking his head gravely. 'I pledge you my professional word I didn't even know she could dance, till her last benefit, and then she played Juliet, and Helen Macgregor, and did the skipping-rope hornpipe between the pieces. The very first time I saw that admirable woman, Johnson,' said Mr Crummles, drawing a little nearer, and speaking in the tone of confidential friendship, 'she stood upon her head on the butt-end of a spear, surrounded with blazing fireworks.'

'You astonish me!' said Nicholas.

'*She* astonished *me*!' returned Mr Crummles, with a very serious countenance. 'Such grace, coupled with such dignity! I adored her from that moment.'

NICHOLAS NICKLEBY, 1838–9

Deformation of Character: Prison, Politics and the Law

Having had first-hand experience of the Marshalsea Prison when his father was sent there for non-payment of debts and, having worked as a lawyer's clerk at Ellis & Blackmore for some time during his late teens, Dickens had a solid grounding when it came to describing both institutions. That he didn't hold either in high esteem (being a long-term campaigner for prison reform as well as a general champion of justice and human decency) ensured that in his novels both the law and the prison system came in for a great deal of criticism as well as a fair amount of lampooning.

Thus, in the midst of the mud, and at the heart of the fog, sits the Lord High Chancellor in his High Court of Chancery.

'Mr Tangle,' says the Lord High Chancellor, latterly something restless under the eloquence of that learned gentleman.

'Mlud,' says Mr Tangle. Mr Tangle knows more of Jarndyce and Jarndyce than anybody. He is famous for it – supposed never to have read anything else since he left school.

'Have you nearly concluded your argument?'

'Mlud, no – variety of points – feel it my duty tsubmit – ludship,' is the reply that slides out of Mr Tangle.

'Several members of the bar are still to be heard, I believe?' says the Chancellor, with a slight smile.

Eighteen of Mr Tangle's learned friends, each armed with a little summary of eighteen hundred sheets, bob up like eighteen hammers in a pianoforte, make eighteen bows, and drop into their eighteen places of obscurity.

'We will proceed with the hearing on Wednesday fortnight,' says the Chancellor. For the question at issue is only a question of costs, a mere bud on the forest tree of the parent suit, and really will come to a settlement one of these days.

BLEAK HOUSE, 1852–3

The Circumlocution Office was (as everybody knows without being told) the most important Department under Government. No public business of any kind could possibly be done at any time, without the acquiescence of the Circumlocution Office. Its finger was in the largest public pie, and in the smallest public tart. It was equally impossible to do the plainest right and to undo the plainest wrong, without the express authority of the Circumlocution Office. If another Gunpowder Plot had been discovered half an hour before the lighting of the match, nobody would have been justified in saving the parliament until there had been half a score of boards, half a bushel of minutes, several sacks of official memoranda, and a family-vault full of ungrammatical correspondence, on the part of the Circumlocution Office . . . Whatever was required to be done, the Circumlocution Office was beforehand with all the public departments in the art of perceiving – HOW NOT TO DO IT.

LITTLE DORRIT, 1855–7

'It was as true . . . as turnips is. It was as true . . . as taxes is. And nothing's truer than them.'
Mr Barkis, *DAVID COPPERFIELD*, 1849–50

'Our member has come down express,' returned the landlord. 'No scrubs would do for no such a purpose. Nothing less would satisfy our Directors than our member in the House of Commons, who is returned upon the Gentlemanly Interest.'

'Which interest is that?' asked Martin.

'What, don't you know!' returned the landlord.

It was quite clear the landlord didn't. They always told him at election time, that it was the Gentlemanly side, and he immediately put on his top-boots, and voted for it.

MARTIN CHUZZLEWIT, 1843–4

'Silence there!' cried the jailer.

'What is this?' inquired one of the magistrates.

'A pick-pocketing case, your worship.'

'Has the boy ever been here before?'

'He ought to have been, a many times,' replied the jailer. 'He has been pretty well everywhere else. *I* know him well, your worship.'

'Oh! you know me, do you?' cried the Artful, making a note of the statement. 'Wery good. That's a case of deformation of character, any way.'

OLIVER TWIST, 1837–9

The mature young gentleman is a gentleman of property. He invests his property. He goes in a condescending, amateurish way into the City, attends meetings of the Directors, and has to do with traffic in Shares. As is well known to the wise in their generation, traffic in Shares is the one thing to have to do with in this world. Have no antecedents, no established character, no cultivation, no ideas, no manners; have Shares. Have Shares enough to be on Boards of Direction in capital letters, oscillate on mysterious business between London and Paris, and be great. Where does he come from? Shares. Where is he going to? Shares. What squeezes him into Parliament? Shares. Perhaps he never of himself achieved success in anything, never originated anything, never produced anything? Sufficient answer to all: Shares. Oh, mighty Shares!

OUR MUTUAL FRIEND, 1864–5

'It is an old prerogative of kings to govern everything but their passions.'
MR PICKWICK, READING FROM 'THE TRUE LEGEND OF PRINCE BLADUD',
THE PICKWICK PAPERS, 1836–7

O h heaven, if you could have been with me at a hospital dinner last Monday! There were men there – your City aristocracy – who made such speeches and expressed such sentiments as any moderately intelligent dustman would have blushed through his cindery bloom to have thought of. Sleek, slobbering, bow-paunched, over-fed, apoplectic, snorting cattle, and the auditory leaping up in their delight! I never saw such an illustration of the power of the purse, or felt so degraded and debased by its contemplation.

LETTER FROM CHARLES DICKENS TO
DOUGLAS JERROLD, 1842

'But you have not imparted to me,' remarks
Veneering, 'what you think of my entering the
House of Commons?'
'I think,' rejoins Twemlow, feelingly, 'that it is the
best club in London.'
OUR MUTUAL FRIEND, 1864–5

'Slumkey forever!' roared the honest and the independent. 'Slumkey forever!' echoed Mr Pickwick, taking off his hat.

'No Fizkin!' roared the crowd.

'Certainly not!' shouted Mr Pickwick.

'Hurrah!' And then there was another roaring, like that of a whole menagerie when the elephant has rung the bell for the cold meat.

'Who is Slumkey?' whispered Mr Tupman.

'I don't know,' replied Mr Pickwick in the same tone.

'Hush. Don't ask any questions. It's always best on these occasions to do what the mob do.'

'But suppose there are two mobs?' suggested Mr Snodgrass.

'Shout with the largest,' replied Mr Pickwick.

Volumes could not have said more.

THE PICKWICK PAPERS, 1836–7

'If there's any illness when that wessel gets to sea,' said Mrs Gamp, prophetically, 'it's murder, and I'm a witness for the persecution.'

MARTIN CHUZZLEWIT, 1843–4

Americans Can't Bear to be Told Their Faults

In January 1842 Charles Dickens, together with his wife, left England for a tour of America. It was a highly successful trip. Dickens was fêted by all and sundry – he met, amongst others, Henry Wadsworth Longfellow and Washington Irving; he attended banquets and balls, gave speeches and had an audience with the then President, John Tyler. 'I can give you no conception of my welcome here,' he wrote to his friend and confidant Thomas Mitton. 'There never was a king or emperor upon the earth so cheered and followed by crowds, and entertained in public at splendid balls and dinners . . .'

But Dickens did not just confine himself to pleasurable pursuits: he also visited mental asylums, prisons, workhouses, orphanages and even an institute for the blind, and he was not disappointed, finding as he did a more modern approach to social welfare than in his own United Kingdom. However, all was not sunshine and light in the New World; indeed there were more than a few hiccups along the way; one arising from Dickens's opinion that British authors were being cheated out of huge sums of money due to the American copyright laws. This led to an immediate outcry by the American press. 'It happens that we want no advice', the *Hartford Times* wrote, 'on the subject and it will be better for Mr Dickens if he refrains from introducing the subject hereafter.'

This war of words continued throughout Dickens's visit and coloured his whole journey through America to the extent that Mary Shelley wrote a letter to a friend saying that 'Charles Dickens has just come home in a state of violent dislike of the Americans – and means to devour them in his next work – he says they are so frightfully dishonest.' His 'next work' was *American Notes*, quickly followed by *Martin Chuzzlewit* – both of which were quite scathing of America.

That being said, Dickens's trip was for the most part an experience that he relished and as he was to comment to John Forster, 'Oh! the sublimated essence of comicality that I *could* distil, from the materials I have!' The following excerpts are a few of Dickens's more humorous observations . . .

I believe that there is no country, on the face of the earth, where there is less freedom of opinion on any subject in reference to which there is a broad difference of opinion than in this . . . There! I write the words with reluctance, disappointment, and sorrow; but I believe it from the bottom of my soul . . . I tremble for a radical coming here, unless he is a radical on principle, by reason and reflection, and from the sense of right. I fear that if he were anything else, he would return home a tory . . . I do fear that the heaviest blow ever dealt at liberty will be dealt by this country, in the failure of its example.

LETTER FROM CHARLES DICKENS TO JOHN FORSTER, 1842

'Is smartness American for forgery?' asked Martin.
'Well! said the colonel, 'I expect it's American for a good many things that you call by other names. But you can't help yourself in Europe. We can.'
'And do, sometimes,' thought Martin.
MARTIN CHUZZLEWIT, 1843–4

In the courts of law, the judge has his spittoon on the bench, the counsel have theirs, the witness has his, the prisoner his, and the crier his. The jury are accommodated at the rate of three men to a spittoon . . . I have twice seen gentlemen at evening parties in New York, turn aside when they were not engaged in conversation, and spit upon the drawing-room carpet. And in every barroom and hotel passage the stone floor looks as if it were paved with open oysters – from the quantity of this kind of deposit which tessellates it all over.

OBSERVATION OF CHARLES DICKENS IN AMERICA, 1842

You can never conceive what the hawking and spitting is, the whole night through. *Upon my honour and word* I was obliged, this morning, to lay my fur-coat on the deck, and wipe the half-dried flakes of spittle from it with my handkerchief: and the only surprise seemed to be, that I should consider it necessary to do so.

LETTER FROM CHARLES DICKENS TO JOHN FORSTER, 1842

There are not so many intensified bores as in these
United States.
OBSERVATION OF CHARLES DICKENS, 1842

I see a press more mean, and paltry, and silly, and disgraceful
than any country I ever knew. . . . I speak of Bancroft, and
am advised to be silent on that subject, for he is 'a black sheep
– a democrat'. I speak of Bryant, and am entreated to be
more careful – for the same reason. I speak of international
copyright, and am implored not to ruin myself outright. I
speak of Miss Martineau, and all parties – Slave Upholders
and Abolitionists, Whigs, Tyler Whigs, and Democrats,
shower down upon her a perfect cataract of abuse.

'But what has she done? Surely she praised America
enough!'

'Yes, but she told us some of our faults, and Americans
can't bear to be told their faults.'
LETTER FROM CHARLES DICKENS
TO WILLIAM CHARLES MACREADY, 1842

I really think my face has acquired a fixed expression of sadness from the constant and unmitigated boring I endure ... There is a line in my chin (on the right side of the underlip) indelibly fixed there by the New Englander ...A dimple has vanished from my cheek, which I felt myself robbed of at the time by a wise legislator.

DICKENS ON HIS VISIT TO AMERICA, 1842

I don't think Anne (Kate's maid) has so much as seen an American tree. She objects to Niagara that, 'it's nothing but water and that there is too much of that.'

AN OBSERVATION OF CHARLES DICKENS ON HIS WIFE'S MAID, ANNE, 1842

Their [the American people's] demeanour is invariably morose, sullen, clownish and repulsive. I should think there is not, on the face of the earth, a people so entirely destitute of humour, vivacity, or the capacity of enjoyment.

OBSERVATION OF CHARLES DICKENS, 1842

Now the coach flung us in a heap on its floor, and now crushed our heads against its roof. . . . Still, the day was beautiful, the air delicious, and we were *alone*, with no tobacco spittle, or eternal prosy conversation about dollars and politics (the only two subjects they ever converse about, or can converse about) to bore us.

OBSERVATION OF CHARLES DICKENS, 1842

Politics are much discussed, so are banks, so is cotton. Quiet people avoid the question of the Presidency . . . the great constitutional feature of this institution being, that directly the acrimony of the last election is over, the next one begins.

AMERICAN NOTES, 1842

In all modes of travelling, the American customs, with reference to the means of personal cleanliness and wholesome ablution, are extremely negligent and filthy; and I strongly incline to the belief that a considerable amount of illness is referable to this cause.

AMERICAN NOTES, 1842

... dyspeptic ladies and gentlemen ... eat unheard-of quantities of hot corn bread (almost as good for the digestion as a kneaded pin-cushion), for breakfast, and for supper. Those who do not observe this custom, and who help themselves several times instead, usually suck their knives and forks meditatively, until they have decided what to take next: then pull them out of their mouths: put them in the dish; help themselves; and fall to work again. At dinner, there is nothing to drink upon the table, but great jugs full of cold water. Nobody says anything, at any meal, to anybody. All the passengers are very dismal, and seem to have tremendous secrets weighing on their minds. There is no conversation, no laughter, no cheerfulness, no sociality, except in spitting; and that is done in silent fellowship round the stove, when the meal is over.

AMERICAN NOTES, 1842

English kindness is very different from American. People send their horses and carriages for your use, but they don't exact as payment the right of being always under your nose.

OBSERVATION OF CHARLES DICKENS, 1842

[B ill] 'All men are alike in the U–nited States, an't they? It makes no odds whether a man has a thousand pound, or nothing, there. Particular in New York, I'm told, where Ned landed.'

'New York, was it?' asked Martin, thoughtfully.

'Yes,' said Bill. 'New York. I know that, because he sent word home that it brought Old York to his mind, quite wivid, in consequence of being so exactly unlike it in every respect.'

MARTIN CHUZZLEWIT, 1843–4

I'm Always Ill After Shakespeare: Books and the Theatre

That Dickens was a novelist who could extract a certain amount of humour from any given subject is unarguable. He saw comedy everywhere and, as several of his close friends attest, his comic observations were not only confined to his novels. There are accounts of Dickens laughing uproariously through dinner parties, of him mimicking friends, relating funny stories and telling jokes, as well as being, when the mood took him, exceedingly sarcastic. For instance when George Henry Lewes (the philosopher, critic and scientist, and partner of George Eliot) wrote a series of articles entitled 'Success in Literature', Dickens responded by saying, 'Success in literature? What on earth does George Lewes know about success in literature?'

However, it *is* to his novels that we turn when we most want to experience Dickens's comic genius and it is no better expressed than when he is poking fun at his own art and those men and women who either worship or denigrate it . . .

'Poetry's unnat'ral; no man ever talked poetry 'cept a beadle on boxin' day, or Warren's blackin' or Rowland's oil, or some o' them low fellows; never you let yourself down to talk poetry, my boy.'
MR WELLER, *THE PICKWICK PAPERS*, 1836–7

Thereupon the Captain, with much alacrity, shouldered his book – for he made it a point of duty to read none but very large books on a Sunday, as having a more staid appearance: and had bargained, years ago, for a prodigious volume at a book-stall, five lines of which utterly confounded him, insomuch that he had not yet ascertained of what subject it treated – and withdrew.
DOMBEY AND SON, 1846–8

'She dotes on poetry, sir. She adores it; I may say that her whole soul and mind are wound up, and entwined with it. She has produced some delightful pieces, herself, sir. You may have met with her "Ode to an Expiring Frog", sir.'
LEO HUNTER, *THE PICKWICK PAPERS*, 1836–7

Cramped in all kinds of dim cupboards and hutches at Tellson's, the oldest of men carried on the business gravely. When they took a young man into Tellson's London house, they hid him somewhere till he was old. They kept him in a dark place, like a cheese, until he had the full Tellson flavour and blue-mould upon him. Then only was he permitted to be seen, spectacularly poring over large books and casting his breeches and gaiters into the general weight of the establishment.

A TALE OF TWO CITIES, 1859

'... vether it's worth while goin' through so much, to learn so little, as the charity-boy said ven he got to the end of the alphabet, is a matter o' taste.'
MR WELLER, *THE PICKWICK PAPERS*, 1836–7

A.D. had no concern with anno Domini, but stood for anno Dombei – and Son.
DOMBEY AND SON, 1846–8

'. . . we have always believed a Secretary to be a piece of furniture, mostly of mahogany, lined with green baize or leather, with a lot of little drawers in it. Now, you won't think I take a liberty when I mention that you certainly ain't *that.*'
MR BOFFIN, *OUR MUTUAL FRIEND*, 1864–5

It was four in the afternoon – that is, the vulgar afternoon of the sun and the clock – and Mrs Wititterly reclined, according to custom, on the drawing-room sofa, while Kate read aloud a new novel in three volumes, entitled 'The Lady Flabella', which Alphonse the doubtful had procured from the library that very morning. And it was a production admirably suited to a lady labouring under Mrs Wititterly's complaint, seeing that there was not a line in it, from beginning to end, which could, by the most remote contingency, awaken the smallest excitement in any person breathing.

NICHOLAS NICKLEBY, 1838–9

'"There's a lot of feet in Shakespeare's verse, but there ain't
any legs worth mentioning in Shakespeare's plays, are there,
Pip? Juliet, Desdemona, Lady Macbeth, and all the rest of
'em, whatever their names are, might as well have no legs at
all, for anything the audience know about it, Pip . . . What's
the legitimate object of the drama, Pip?
Human nature. What are legs? Human nature. Then let
us have plenty of leg pieces, Pip . . ."'
MR PIP, QUOTING 'THE VISCOUNT',
MARTIN CHUZZLEWIT, 1843–4

'Mr Bazzard's father, being a Norfolk farmer, would have
furiously laid about him with a flail, a pitch-fork, and every
agricultural implement available for assaulting purposes, on
the slightest hint of his son's having written a play.'
MR GREWGIOUS, *THE MYSTERY OF EDWIN DROOD*, 1870

'I'm always ill after Shakespeare.'
MRS WITITTERLY, *NICHOLAS NICKLEBY*, 1838–9

'. . . a literary man – *with* a wooden leg – is always liable
to jealousy.'
MR BOFFIN, *OUR MUTUAL FRIEND*, 1864–5

'Well, sir,' returned Mr Tapley, 'sooner than you
should do that, I'll com-ply. It's a considerable
invasion of a man's jollity to be made so
partickler welcome, but a Werb is a word as
signifies to be, to do, or to suffer (which is all
the grammar, and enough too, as ever I wos
taught); and if there's a Werb alive, I'm it. For
I'm always a-bein', sometimes a-doin', and
continually a-sufferin'.'
MARTIN CHUZZLEWIT, 1843–4

No one who can read, ever looks at a book, even unopened
on a shelf, like one who cannot.
OUR MUTUAL FRIEND, 1864–5

'. . . there are books of which the backs and covers are by
far the best parts.'
MR BROWNLOW, *OLIVER TWIST*, 1837–9

Tired of working, and conversing with Miss Twinkleton, she
suggested working and reading: to which Miss Twinkleton
readily assented, as an admirable reader, of
tried powers. But Rosa soon made the discovery that Miss
Twinkleton didn't read fairly. She cut the love-scenes,
interpolated passages in praise of female celibacy, and was
guilty of other glaring pious frauds.
THE MYSTERY OF EDWIN DROOD, 1870

Please, Sir . . .
I Want
Some More

In an age when half the population were either starving to death or fed on such delicacies as gruel, it is hardly surprising that many of Dickens's novels use food as a means of highlighting social iniquity. Of course the scene in *Oliver Twist* where Oliver 'asks for more' is now etched into the collective consciousness, but there are several other scenes in Dickens's novels that combine both humour and pathos where food is concerned – in *David Copperfield*, for instance, where the naïve young boy is cheated out of his meal by a very unscrupulous waiter.

'Please, sir,' replied Oliver, 'I want some more.'

The master aimed a blow at Oliver's head with the ladle; pinioned him in his arms; and shrieked aloud for the beadle.

The board were sitting in solemn conclave, when Mr Bumble rushed into the room in great excitement, and addressing the gentleman in the high chair, said, 'Mr Limbkins, I beg your pardon, sir! Oliver Twist has asked for more!'

There was a general start. Horror was depicted on every countenance.

'For *more*!' said Mr Limbkins. 'Compose yourself, Bumble, and answer me distinctly. Do I understand that he asked for more, after he had eaten the supper allotted by the dietary?'

'He did, sir,' replied Bumble.

'That boy will be hung,' said the gentleman in the white waistcoat. 'I know that boy will be hung.'

OLIVER TWIST, 1837–9

Mr Pecksniff promptly departed, followed by Mrs Gamp, who, seeing that he took a bottle and glass from the cupboard, and carried it in his hand, was much softened.

MARTIN CHUZZLEWIT, 1843–4

'Tell Mrs Gamp to come up-stairs,' said Mould. 'Now Mrs Gamp, what's *your* news?'

The lady in question was by this time in the doorway, curtseying to Mrs Mould. At the same moment a peculiar fragrance was borne upon the breeze, as if a passing fairy had hiccoughed, and had previously been to a wine-vault.

MARTIN CHUZZLEWIT, 1843–4

'It's not Madness, ma'am,' replied Mr Bumble, after a few moments of deep meditation. 'It's Meat.'

'What?' exclaimed Mrs Sowerberry.

'Meat, ma'am, meat,' replied Bumble, with stern emphasis. 'You've over-fed him . . . If you had kept the boy on gruel, ma'am, this would never have happened.'

'Dear, dear!' ejaculated Mrs Sowerberry, piously raising her eyes to the kitchen ceiling: 'this comes of being liberal!'

OLIVER TWIST, 1837–9

'Tongue; well, that's a wery good thing when it
ain't a woman's.'
Mr Weller, *The Pickwick Papers*, 1836–7

'There's half a pint of ale for you. Will you have it now?'
I thanked him and said, 'Yes.' Upon which he poured
it out of a jug into a large tumbler, and held it up against the
light, and made it look beautiful.

'My eye!' he said. 'It seems a good deal, don't it?'

'It does seem a good deal,' I answered with a smile. For it
was quite delightful to me, to find him so pleasant. He was
a twinkling-eyed, pimple-faced man, with his hair standing
upright all over his head; and as he stood with one arm
a-kimbo, holding up the glass to the light with the other hand,
he looked quite friendly.

'There was a gentleman here, yesterday,' he said – 'a stout
gentleman, by the name of Topsawyer – perhaps you know
him?'

'No,' I said, 'I don't think – '

'In breeches and gaiters, broad-brimmed hat, grey coat,
speckled choker,' said the waiter.

'No,' I said bashfully, 'I haven't the pleasure – '

'He came in here,' said the waiter, looking at the light through the tumbler, 'ordered a glass of this ale – *would* order it – I told him not – drank it, and fell dead. It was too old for him. It oughtn't to be drawn; that's the fact.'

I was very much shocked to hear of this melancholy accident, and said I thought I had better have some water.

'Why, you see,' said the waiter, still looking at the light through the tumbler, with one of his eyes shut up, 'our people don't like things being ordered and left. It offends 'em. But I'll drink it, if you like. I'm used to it, and use is everything. I don't think it'll hurt me, if I throw my head back, and take it off quick. Shall I?'

I replied that he would much oblige me by drinking it, if he thought he could do it safely, but by no means otherwise. When he did throw his head back, and take it off quick, I had a horrible fear, I confess, of seeing him meet the fate of the lamented Mr Topsawyer, and fall lifeless on the carpet. But it didn't hurt him. On the contrary, I thought he seemed the fresher for it.

'What have we got here?' he said, putting a fork into my dish. 'Not chops?'

'Chops,' I said.

'Lord bless my soul!' he exclaimed, 'I didn't know they were chops. Why, a chop's the very thing to take off the bad effects of that beer! Ain't it lucky?'

So he took a chop by the bone in one hand, and a potato in the other, and ate away with a very good appetite, to my extreme satisfaction. He afterwards took another chop, and another potato; and after that, another chop and another potato. When we had done, he brought me a pudding, and having set it before me, seemed to ruminate, and to become absent in his mind for some moments.

'How's the pie?' he said, rousing himself.

'It's a pudding,' I made answer.

'Pudding!' he exclaimed. 'Why, bless me, so it is! What!' looking at it nearer. 'You don't mean to say it's a batter-pudding!'

'Yes, it is indeed.'

'Why, a batter-pudding,' he said, taking up a tablespoon, 'is my favourite pudding! Ain't that lucky? Come on, little 'un, and let's see who'll get most.'

The waiter certainly got most. He entreated me more than once to come in and win, but what with his tablespoon to my tea-spoon, his dispatch to my dispatch, and his appetite to my appetite, I was left far behind at the first mouthful, and had no chance with him. I never saw anyone enjoy a pudding so much, I think; and he laughed, when it was all gone, as if his enjoyment of it lasted still.

[...]

It was a little disconcerting for me to find, when I was being helped up behind the coach, that I was supposed to have eaten all the dinner without any assistance. I discovered this, from overhearing the lady in the bow-window say to the guard, 'Take care of that child, George, or he'll burst!' and from observing that the women-servants who were about the place came out to look and giggle at me as a young phenomenon. My unfortunate friend the waiter, who had quite recovered his spirits, did not appear to be disturbed by this, but joined in the general admiration without being at all confused. If I had any doubt of him, I suppose this half awakened it; but I am inclined to believe that with the simple confidence of a child, and the natural reliance of a child upon superior years (qualities I am very sorry any children should prematurely change for worldly wisdom), I had no serious mistrust of him on the whole, even then.

DAVID, *DAVID COPPERFIELD*, 1849–50

Papa, Potatoes, Poultry, Prunes and Prism: Nonsenses

That there are so many humorous moments in Dickens's novels makes it well-nigh impossible to include each and every one – however, below are a few of the choicest moments . . .

'Terrible place – dangerous work – other day – five children – mother – tall lady, eating sandwiches – forgot the arch – crash – knock – children look round – mother's head off – sandwich in her hand – no mouth to put it in – head of a family off – shocking, shocking!'
THE PICKWICK PAPERS, 1836–7

'Do you know, now,' said Mr Pecksniff, folding his hands, and looking at his young relation with an air of pensive interest, 'that I should very much like to see your notion of a cowhouse?'

But Martin by no means appeared to relish this suggestion.

'A pump,' said Mr Pecksniff, 'is a very chaste practice. I have found that a lamp-post is calculated to refine the mind and give it a classical tendency. An ornamental turnpike has a remarkable effect upon the imagination. What do you say to beginning with an ornamental turnpike?'
MARTIN CHUZZLEWIT, 1843–4

'I am sure there was a case in the day before yesterday's paper, extracted from one of the French newspapers, about a journeyman shoemaker who was jealous of a young girl in an adjoining village, because she wouldn't shut herself up in an airtight three-pair of stairs, and charcoal herself to death with him; and who went and hid himself in a wood with a sharp-pointed knife, and rushed out, as she was passing by with a few friends, and killed himself first, and then all the friends, and then her – no, killed all the friends first, and then herself and then *him*self – which it is quite frightful to think of. Somehow or other,' added Mrs Nickleby, after a momentary pause, 'they always *are* journeyman shoemakers who do these things in France, according to the papers. I don't know how it is – something in the leather, I suppose.'

MRS NICKLEBY, *NICHOLAS NICKLEBY*, 1838–9

'Something will come of this. I hope it mayn't be human gore!'
SIMON TAPPERTIT, *BARNABY RUDGE*, 1841,
ON GRINDING UP TOOLS

'. . . Take another glass of wine, and excuse my mentioning that society as a body does not expect one to be so strictly conscientious in emptying one's glass, as to turn it bottom upwards with the rim on one's nose.'
HERBERT POCKET, *GREAT EXPECTATIONS*, 1860-1

When you have parted with a man, at two o'clock in the morning, on terms of the utmost good fellowship, and he meets you again, at half-past nine, and greets you as a serpent, it is not unreasonable to conclude that something of an unpleasant nature has occurred meanwhile.
THE PICKWICK PAPERS, 1836–7

'There are only two styles of portrait painting; the serious and the smirk.'
MISS LA CREEVY, *NICHOLAS NICKLEBY*, 1838–9

DOTHEBOYS HALL,
THURSDAY MORNING

Sir, My pa requests me to write to you. The doctors consider it doubtful whether he will ever recuvver the use of his legs which prevents his holding a pen.

We are in a state of mind byond everything, and my pa is one mask of brooses both blue and green likewise two forms are steepled in his Goar. We were kimpelled to have him carried down into the kitchen where he now lays. You will judge from this that he has been brought very low.

When your nevew that you recommended for a teacher had done this to my pa and jumped upon his body with his feet and also langwedge which I will not pollewt my pen with describing, he assaulted my ma with dreadful violence, dashed her to the earth, and drove her back comb several inches into her head. A very little more and it must have entered her skull. We have a medical certifiket that if it had, the tortershell would have affected the brain . . .

I remain

    Yours and cetrer

      Fanny Squeers

P.S. I pity his ignorance and despise him.

NICHOLAS NICKLEBY, 1838–9

'Papa, potatoes, poultry, prunes and prism, are all very good words for the lips; especially prunes and prism.'
MRS GENERAL, *LITTLE DORRIT*, 1855–7

The one great principle of the English law is to make business for itself.
BLEAK HOUSE, 1852–3

'It's over, and can't be helped, and that's one consolation, as they always says in Turkey, ven they cuts the wrong man's head off.'
SAM WELLER, *THE PICKWICK PAPERS*, 1836–7

I never had anything left to me but relations.
OBSERVATION OF CHARLES DICKENS FOLLOWING THE DEATH OF HIS BROTHER, ALFRED, WHOSE FAMILY CHARLES WAS LEFT TO LOOK AFTER, 1860

... Mr and Mrs Boffin sat staring at mid-air, and Mrs Wilfer
sat silently giving them to understand that every breath
she drew required to be drawn with a self-denial rarely
paralleled in history ...
OUR MUTUAL FRIEND, 1864–5

'Ah! you should keep dogs – fine animals – sagacious
creatures – dog of my own once – Pointer – surprising
instinct – out shooting one day – entering inclosure –
whistled – dog stopped – whistled again – Ponto – no go;
stock still – called him – Ponto, Ponto – wouldn't move – dog
transfixed – staring at a board – looked up, saw an inscription
– "Gamekeeper has orders to shoot all dogs found in this
inclosure" – wouldn't pass it – wonderful dog – valuable dog
that – very.'

'THE STRANGER' (MR JINGLE),
THE PICKWICK PAPERS, 1836–7

'Here's the rule for bargains: "Do other men, for they
would do you." That's the true business precept.
All others are counterfeits.'
JONAS CHUZZLEWIT, *MARTIN CHUZZLEWIT*, 1843–4

'There can be no doubt,' said Mrs Nickleby, 'that he *is* a gentleman, and has the manners of a gentleman, and the appearance of a gentleman, although he does wear smalls and grey worsted stockings. That may be eccentricity, or he may be proud of his legs. I don't see why he shouldn't be. The Prince Regent was proud of his legs, and so was Daniel Lambert, who was also a fat man; *he* was proud of his legs. So was Miss Biffin: she was – no,' added Mrs Nickleby, correcting herself, 'I think she had only toes, but the principle is the same.'

NICHOLAS NICKLEBY, 1838–9

'Many and many is the circuit this pony has gone,' said Mr Crummles, flicking him skilfully on the eyelid for old acquaintance' sake. 'He is quite one of us. His mother was on the stage.'

'Was she, indeed?' rejoined Nicholas.

'She ate apple-pie at a circus for upwards of fourteen years,' said the manager; 'fired pistols, and went to bed in a nightcap; and, in short, took the low comedy entirely. His father was a dancer.'

'Was he at all distinguished?'

'Not very,' said the manager. 'He was rather a low sort of pony. The fact is, he had been originally jobbed out by the day, and he never quite got over his old habits. He was clever in melodrama too, but too broad – too broad. When the mother died, he took the port-wine business.'

'The port-wine business!' cried Nicholas.

'Drinking port-wine with the clown,' said the manager; 'but he was greedy, and one night bit off the bowl of the glass, and choked himself, so that his vulgarity was the death of him at last.'

NICHOLAS NICKLEBY, 1838–9

...**M**rs Gamp took him by the collar of his coat, and gave some dozen or two of hearty shakes backward and forward in his chair; that exercise being considered by the disciples of the Prig school of nursing (who are very numerous among professional ladies) as exceedingly conducive to repose, and highly beneficial to the performance of nervous functions. Its effect in this instance was to render the patient so giddy and addle-headed, that he could say nothing more; which Mrs Gamp regarded as the triumph of her art.

'There!' she said, loosening the old man's cravat, in consequence of his being rather black in the face, after this scientific treatment. 'Now, I hope, you're easy in your mind. If you should turn at all faint we can soon revive you, sir, I promige you. Bite a person's thumbs, or turn their fingers the wrong way,' said Mrs Gamp, smiling with the consciousness of at once imparting pleasure and instruction to her auditors, 'and they comes to, wonderful, Lord bless you!'

MARTIN CHUZZLEWIT, 1843–4

It is one of the easiest achievements in life to offend your family when your family want to get rid of you.
Our Mutual Friend, 1864–5

'Hackney coaches, my lord, are such nasty things, that it's almost better to walk at any time, for although I believe a hackney coachman can be transported for life, if he has a broken window, still they are so reckless, that they nearly all have broken windows. I once had a swelled face for six weeks, my lord, from riding in a hackney coach – I think it was a hackney coach,' said Mrs Nickleby reflecting, 'though I'm not quite certain whether it wasn't a chariot; at all events I know it was dark green, with a very long number, beginning with a nought and ending with a nine – no, beginning with a nine, and ending with a nought, that was it, and of course the stamp office people would know at once whether it was a coach or a chariot if any inquiries were made there – however that was, there it was with a broken window and there was I for six weeks with a swelled face . . .'.

NICHOLAS NICKLEBY, 1838–9

. . . still his philanthropy was of that gunpowderous sort that
the difference between it and animosity was hard
to determine.
THE MYSTERY OF EDWIN DROOD, 1870,
OF MR HONEYTHUNDER

'...Your grandmother, Kate, was exactly the same – precisely. The least excitement, the slightest surprise, she fainted away directly. I have heard her say, often and often, that when she was a young lady, and before she was married, she was turning a corner into Oxford Street one day, when she ran against her own hairdresser, who, it seems, was escaping from a bear; – the mere suddenness of the encounter made her faint away directly. Wait, though,' added Mrs Nickleby, pausing to consider. 'Let me be sure I'm right. Was it her hairdresser who had escaped from a bear, or was it a bear who had escaped from her hairdresser's? I declare I can't remember just now, but the hairdresser was a very handsome man, I know, and quite a gentleman in his manners; so that it has nothing to do with the point of the story.'

NICHOLAS NICKLEBY, 1838–9

There were three other Young Barnacles, from three other offices, insipid to all the senses, and terribly in want of seasoning, doing the marriage as they would have 'done' the Nile, Old Rome ... or Jerusalem.

LITTLE DORRIT, 1855–7

Reginald Wilfer is a name with rather a grand sound, suggesting on first acquaintance, brasses in country churches, scrolls in stained-glass windows, and generally the De Wilfers who came over with the Conqueror. For, it is a remarkable fact in genealogy that no De Anyones ever came over with Anybody else.

OUR MUTUAL FRIEND, 1864–5

'There is no such passion in human nature, as the passion for gravy among commercial gentlemen.'

MRS TODGERS, *MARTIN CHUZZLEWIT*, 1843–4

'Dead!' replied the other, with a contemptuous emphasis. 'Not he. You won't catch Ned a-dying easy. No, no. He knows better than that.'

BILL SIMMONS, *MARTIN CHUZZLEWIT*, 1843–4

Works by Charles Dickens

NOVELS

The Pickwick Papers (1836-7)
Oliver Twist (1837-9)
Nicholas Nickleby (1838-9)
The Old Curiosity Shop (1840-1)
Barnaby Rudge (1841)
Martin Chuzzlewit (1843-4)
A Christmas Carol (1843)
Dombey and Son (1846-8)
David Copperfield (1848-50)
Bleak House (1851-3)
Hard Times (1854)
Little Dorrit (1855-7)
A Tale of Two Cities (1859)
Great Expectations (1860-1)
Our Mutual Friend (1864-5)
The Mystery of Edwin Drood (1870)

NON-FICTION

A Child's History of England
American Notes
Pictures from Italy

SHORT STORIES AND ESSAYS

'A Christmas Tree'
'A Message from the Sea'
'Doctor Marigold'
'George Silverman's Explanation'
'Going Into Society'
'Holiday Romance'
'Hunted Down'
'Mrs Lirriper's Legacy'
'Mrs Lirriper's Logdings'
'Mugby Junction'
'Perils of Certain English Prisoners'
'Somebody's Luggage'
'Sunday Under Three Heads'
'The Child's Story'
'The Haunted House'
'The Haunted Man and the Ghost's Bargain'
'The Holly-Tree'
'The Lamplighter'
'The Poor Relation's Story'
'The Schoolboy's Story'
'The Seven Poor Travellers'
'The Signal-Man'
'The Trial for Murder'
'Tom Tiddler's Ground'
'What Christmas Is As We Grow Older'
'Wreck of the Golden Mary'